The DIY Bride

An Affair to Remember

40 Fantastic Projects to Celebrate Your Unique Wedding Style

KHRIS COCHRAN

A Stonesong Press Book

The Taunton Press

To my two guys, Jason and Zion: I thank you for your never-ending love and support.
You make life sweeter and continue to expand my definition of love and happiness.
To my in-laws, Blythe and Russ: May your generosity and kindness be returned to you tenfold.
Without your support, assembly skills, and babysitting sessions, this book would not have been possible.

Text © 2012 by The Stonesong Press, LLC and Khris Cochran
Photographs © 2012 by The Stonesong Press, LLC
Illustrations © 2012 by The Stonesong Press, LLC

The Taunton Press
Inspiration for hands-on living®

The Taunton Press, Inc., 63 South Main Street, P.O. Box 5506, Newtown, CT 06470-5506
e-mail: tp@taunton.com
Editors: Erica Sanders-Foege, Christina Glennon
Copy editor: Valerie J. Cimino
Indexer: Cathy Goddard
Jacket/Cover design: 3 & Co.
Interior design: Teresa Fernandes
Layout: Cathy Cassidy
Illustrator: Alexis Seabrook
Photographer: Jack Deutsch
Stylists: Laura Mafeo, Julie Hines

A Stonesong Press Book
CraftStylish™ is a trademark of The Taunton Press, Inc., registered in the U.S. Patent and Trademark Office.

The following names/manufacturers appearing in *DIY Bride An Affair to Remember* are trademarks: Adobe Photoshop™ or Adobe Photoshop Elements™, Cheerios™, Chex®, Command™, Craigslist℠, Creative Paperclay®, eBay®, Etsy℠, Facebook℠, Flickr℠, Goo Gone®, Google®, Hobby Lobby℠, Hoyle®, IKEA®, iPod℠, Jo-Ann Fabrics and Crafts℠, Kinko's℠, Krylon® Looking Glass® Mirror-Like Paint, Life Savers®, Liquid Nails®, Michael's℠, Microsoft® Word, Pepto-Bismol®, Perfect Paper Adhesive™, Play-Doh®, Solderite™, Target℠, Walmart℠, X-ACTO™

Library of Congress Cataloging-in-Publication Data

Cochran, Khris.
  The DIY bride, an affair to remember : 40 fantastic projects to celebrate
your unique wedding style / Khris Cochran.
     p. cm.
  ISBN 978-1-60085-351-7 (pbk.)
  1. Handicraft. 2. Wedding decorations. I. Title. II. Title:
Do-it-yourself bride, an affair to remember. III. Title: Affair to remember.
  TT149.C5833 2012
  745.594'1--dc23
                        2011034933
Printed in the United States of America
10 9 8 7 6 5 4 3 2 1

About Your Safety: Using tools improperly or ignoring safety practices can lead to permanent injury or even death. Don't try to perform operations you learn about here (or elsewhere) unless you're certain they are safe for you. If something about an operation doesn't feel right, don't do it. Look for another way. We want you to enjoy the craft, so please keep safety foremost in your mind.

Acknowledgments

This book, like a marriage, has brought together a whole community of people who are dedicated to supporting its success.

I could not have done this without the sheer awesomeness of the team at The Stonesong Press. Alison Fargis, Ellen Scordato, Katherine Latshaw, and Nola Solomon went above and beyond to make *An Affair to Remember* a reality. For their infinite patience and understanding as things fell apart on my end, for all of the creative input, editing prowess, and gentle guidance, I am forever grateful.

The dynamic duo of photographer Jack Deutsch and stylist Laura Maffeo have taken 40 craft projects and turned them into book-worthy pieces of art. It is an honor to have their work as part of this book.

My sincerest and wholehearted thanks goes to the entire team at The Taunton Press, including my editors, Erica Sanders-Foege and Christina Glennon, for believing in DIY Bride and for extending, once again, the opportunity to create something wonderful together.

Contents

Introduction

The inspiration for this book was you, dear reader. Many months ago—years now, actually—in brainstorming sessions about what my next DIY Bride book would be, I kept returning to today's DIY couple: Who are modern do-it-yourselfers? What information and crafts do they most seek out? How do they go about planning their weddings? How can DIY Bride better address their needs in ways we haven't done before?

When I wrote *The DIY Bride: 40 Fun Projects for Your Ultimate One-of-a-Kind Wedding* in 2006, the do-it-yourself wedding landscape was much different than it is today. As the years have progressed, the average crafter has changed. Where once DIY was relegated to micro-budget weddings, it's now a fixture in more than half of all weddings, micro, mid-range, and luxury budgets included. Couples are now craftier from the outset thanks to several years of explosive DIY and craft movements. The Internet has fostered strong DIY communities and has helped create a DIY-based economy where crafters can easily find and buy unique do-it-yourself supplies from both big box and independent sellers. It's such an exciting time to be a do-it-yourselfer because so many wedding and craft resources are readily available to you like never before!

The DIY Bride and my follow-up title, *The DIY Bride Crafty Countdown: 40 Fabulous Projects to Make in the Months, Weeks & Hours Before Your Special Day,* focused on basic crafting skills and how to best schedule crafting into the already far too busy schedule of engaged couples. *The DIY Bride An Affair to Remember* takes a step back by addressing a fundamental question about how you plan a wedding, which is usually by style or location. So much of what you'll craft is based on these two points that it made sense to pull some of the most popular themes into one how-to book.

Chapter One covers all things nautical. If your big day involves boats, docks, lakes, beach, oceans, or other beside-the-seaside goodness, this chapter is for you.

Chapter Two presents a modern fairy-tale wedding, combining romance and glamour without being too frou-frou.

For couples with a touch of wanderlust, Chapter Three is dedicated to you. These projects were designed to travel to destinations exotic or familiar—or to just make your guests feel like they've been transported to paradise.

One of my favorite themes, the winter wedding, fills out Chapter Four. For those of you hosting cold-weather nuptials, this chapter will get you started with cozy winter wonderland ideas.

If rustic chic and country charm are more your style, Chapter Five presents projects that are perfectly suited to a sweet country wedding.

For those who want to pay homage to the landmarks and quirky places that help define the soul of the city, Chapter Six will be your go-to.

Into the garden we go in Chapter Seven. These projects are perfect for intimate outdoor or floral-themed weddings.

Chapter Eight takes modern wedding themes beyond just clean lines and minimalism. It's all about combining modern elements with unusual textures, materials, and even a sense of the past to create something fresh and unique.

In *An Affair To Remember,* my goal is to provide you with 40 projects that fit my ultimate DIY criteria:

- They must be affordable.
- Supplies must be readily available.
- They must be adaptable to a number of styles.
- They can fit into the already harried schedules of busy working couples.
- Nearly anyone can complete them no matter what their level of craftiness.

It's a tall order, but I think the diversity of projects will inspire your own crafty masterpieces, no matter what your site or theme.

The mission of DIY Bride—and this book—is to empower you to be an active participant in your wedding, to create the dream wedding you've imagined, no matter what your budget or skill level. In my experience the truly beautiful and meaningful weddings are the ones that the couple have taken a genuine interest in creating themselves.

I know for many couples the idea of getting hands-on can be intimidating, but it doesn't have to be. A DIY wedding can be affordable, easy, and fun. I cover nearly everything you and your beloved will need for the wedding, from the essential elements like save-the-dates, invitations, and favors to grand projects like beautiful fresh floral bouquets and a multitiered silk-covered cupcake stand.

With each project I share hints to help ensure your craft's success with suggestions for saving time and money, how to further customize a project, and a nifty Resources section (see page 216) for finding supplies. All of these features are designed to take away any apprehension you may have and replace it with the sense of adventure and accomplishment that having a personalized wedding can bring. If you're still feeling a bit intimidated or overwhelmed, please drop by www.diybride.com. In addition to a multitude of tutorials, downloads, and classes, we have a community of do-it-yourselfers who are eager to share their knowledge and kindness with you. You've got a built-in support system with us, and we can't wait to welcome you!

The Basics: The DIY BRIDE'S Tools

One of the most daunting tasks in becoming a rock star do-it-yourselfer is putting together a crafter's tool kit. This tool kit is going to be your best buddy during the crafting process, so it's important to choose wisely. A good tool will make your projects easier and serve you well for years; a not-so-good tool can totally sabotage a project and obliterate your budget. After years of being a professional crafter—and having blown thousands of my own dollars on plenty of those not-so-good tools—I know from first-hand experience the importance of a good tool kit.

Most common craft tools and supplies are found at local stores or online. Major craft retailers such as Michael's℠, Jo-Ann's℠, and Hobby Lobby℠ carry a large collection of basic tools and supplies. Large discount department stores like Target℠ and Walmart℠ now have whole areas dedicated to craft products. And don't forget the online craft universe. The Resources section of this book (see page 216) features a handy list of great retailers to help you on your search for the best tools on a budget.

Essential Tools and Supplies

Adhesives

Double-sided tape: This clear tape has adhesive on both sides for quick and easy bonding. It adheres instantly and will not bleed through or buckle paper. Use it in place of glue for paper projects.

Glue gun and glue sticks: Trigger-fed glue guns heat solid glue sticks and dispense the melted glue. They provide a near-instant bond and are perfect for adhering non-paper materials such as silk flowers, lace, ribbon, and more. (Caution: Hot glue will sometimes bleed through lightweight papers and fabrics.) Glue sticks come in two basic types: low-temperature and regular-temperature. Low-temperature glue heats at a lower temperature, perfect if you're new to using a glue gun or, if like me, you tend to burn yourself. Low-temperature glues will take longer to reach their full liquid (and usability) state and often take longer to bond.

Spray adhesive: An aerosol glue, spray adhesive is one of my favorite tools for crafting. It's best used for adhering paper to paper or paper to fabric. It creates a permanent bond, adheres very quickly, and dries clear. Remember to always use it in a well-ventilated space.

Cutting Tools

Craft knife: Also known by the brand name X-ACTO™ knife, this pencil-like tool has a sharp, single-edged knife at the end. It's best for cutting ornate designs on paper, vellum, and other lightweight materials. Heavy-duty versions are also available for cutting thicker materials such as chipboard and balsa wood.

Cutting mat: Self-healing cutting mats are used in conjunction with craft knives and rotary cutters. Their smooth surface repairs itself after a cut, leaving an even cutting area for your next project. Most feature ruled lines on the surface to make cutting and measuring a snap.

Paper cutter: Use this tool for making straight cuts on paper. Most styles have either a removable sliding blade or a rotary blade with built-in measuring grids and/or rulers. Do be sure to have extra blades on hand.

Rotary cutter: A rotary cutter looks and acts much like a pizza wheel. It will cut fabric or paper as it rolls over the surface, which allows you to make a long, straight cut in a single movement.

Pinking shears: Used on fabrics to help prevent fraying and on paper for decorative purposes, pinking shears are scissors with sawtooth blades instead of the straight blades of a standard pair of scissors.

Scissors: A good pair of general-purpose scissors will make your life easier, so invest in the best pair you can afford. A 5-in. to 8-in. stainless steel pair will last for decades with minimum maintenance and will be suitable for most craft projects.

Embroidery and Sewing

All-purpose thread: Polyester or cotton-wrapped polyester thread is used for hand and machine sewing on most fabrics.

Embroidery floss: A bundle of six strands of thread that is loosely twisted together, most embroidery floss comes in cotton, silk, or rayon.

Embroidery needle: Similar to a standard needle, embroidery needles have a longer eye to accommodate thicker embroidery threads and yarns.

Fray preventer: To help prevent the edges of a fabric from unraveling or fraying, liquid fray retarders are available in small point-tipped bottles at fabric and craft stores.

Iron: A heavy-duty household iron is essential for all of your fabric projects.

Needles: For hand-sewn projects, have on hand a selection of needle sizes.

Pins: Use pins with plastic or glass heads; they're easy to see.

Sewing machine: There are small, inexpensive "craft" sewing machines on the market, but you're better off using a regular sewing machine. They're typically more reliable and sturdier, and that will save you a ton of frustration.

Floral

Floral shears: Designed for deadheading, shaping, and pruning cut flowers without damaging the plant, a good pair of floral shears will feature a compact design and stainless steel blades.

Floral tape: A thin, non-sticky tape that only becomes self-adhesive when stretched. Because of this, it's ideal for wrapping flower stems without it becoming a tangled mess. Floral tape comes in brown, green, and white and usually in $\frac{1}{4}$-in. widths.

Floral wire: Generally available in thicknesses from 24 gauge to 16 gauge (thinnest to thickest), floral wires are used to wire bunches of flowers together or in place of a flower's stem to allow for better maneuverability of a bud within an arrangement.

Wire cutters: Floral wires require a hardware-grade wire cutter—not something you'd use for jewelry. A good pair of wire cutters will last you a lifetime, so choose a mid- to high-end pair.

Rubber Stamping and Block Printing

Art stamps: Using art stamps is an easy way to add graphics to your projects. There are two common types on the market: rubber and acrylic. Rubber stamps are opaque; acrylic stamps are transparent. Both types will imprint images, words, or patterns on nearly any surface and are available in countless designs and sizes.

Baren: This is a round tool with a smooth, flat surface that provides a friction-free way to transfer an image from a linoleum block to a piece of paper without smudging.

Block printing ink: Specifically for the linoleum print technique, these inks have a thick, rich consistency and are opaque. Most are oil-based and do require extended drying time.

Brayer: This is a roller with a handle that is used to apply ink to a rubber stamp or a printing block. It provides a uniform coat of ink to large stamp surfaces.

Rubber stamping ink: For rubber stamps, ink is used with an ink pad. While there are several types of inks to choose from, two types will carry you through most of your projects:

Dye Inks: Dye-based inks are water-based and permanent. They dry quickly and can be used on all paper types. Their fast drying time makes them unsuitable for embossing.

Pigment Ink: Pigment-based inks are thicker, more vibrant, and slower to dry than dye-based inks. They can be used on any paper but will smudge when wet. Their slow drying time makes them perfect for use with embossing powders.

Paper Crafts

Bone folder: Bone folders are used to smooth, score, and crease paper. Traditionally, they've been made of polished cow bone. Today you can find heavy acrylic versions at craft and stationery stores.

Die punch: This small steel column has holes and a punch at one end used to make holes. They come in a variety of shapes and sizes and can be found at hardware or craft stores.

Die-cutting machine: Used primarily for cutting thin, flat materials, a die-cutting machine punches shapes out of paper or can be used to emboss text, patterns, or textures into thick cardstock.

Precious Metal Clay

Acrylic rolling pin: Usually found in the clay sections of craft stores, acrylic rolling pins are about 8 in. long and 1 in. in diameter. The smooth, firm surface helps ensure the clay is free from indentations or imperfections when rolled out.

Butane torch: This small, refillable torch is used for firing precious metal clay. These can be found in hardware stores in the soldering sections or in kitchen departments at your favorite department store, cleverly disguised as crème brûlée torches.

Firing block: You'll need a barrier to protect your furniture or work surface during the firing process, since you'll be working with extremely high temperatures. Firing blocks or soldering blocks can be found at some hardware stores or online at precious metal clay retailers.

Jewelry files: These are available in 4- to 10-piece sets at your local craft or jewelry supply shops. When working with precious metal clay, it's best to have a variety of file sizes and surfaces, from gritty to fine.

Steel brush: Available from your local hardware store, a small steel bristle brush is used to remove residue left over from the fired clay firing process.

Silver Leaf

Silver leaf: Wax paper–backed sheets of real silver are pounded into wafer-thin sheets to create silver leaf.

Silver leaf sizing: This is a slow-drying adhesive specifically designed for use with silver and gold leafing.

General

In addition to the specialty tools listed, I recommend the following tools, which you're probably already familiar with:

- #2 pencils
- Acrylic paint
- Cellophane tape
- Emery boards
- Extra craft knife blades
- Gum erasers
- Hammer
- Paint markers
- Permanent markers
- Ruler and straightedge
- Sponge paint brushes
- White pencil

Troubleshooting

An inevitable part of the crafting experience is that things will go awry. This is a quick guide to help with the most common problems that you may encounter when creating the projects in this book.

ADHESIVES

PROBLEM: Layered paper projects fall apart.

CAUSES: The tape is too weak for heavy cardstock, or it is old or of poor quality. Humidity may be affecting the tape's adhesive. The layers have not been burnished (pressed together) properly.

SOLUTIONS: Using a bone folder or the back of a spoon, press the layers together again, or try new or stronger tape.

PROBLEM: Spray adhesive is not adhering properly.

CAUSES: The adhesive has not had enough time to set or is "temporary" hold and not permanent bond.

SOLUTION: Make certain that you are using permanent bond spray adhesive.

FLORAL PROJECTS

PROBLEM: My flowers are droopy or wilted.

CAUSES: The flowers have not been properly stored or hydrated, or they are too hot or too cold.

SOLUTIONS: Some flowers can be revived by placing them in cold water and storing them in a cool room for a while so they can rehydrate. It's best to store flowers in a cool room; anything under 60 degrees F is usually ideal (think air-conditioned room, large refrigerator, or basement) to protect your investment. Should your blooms not perk up, grocery stores are often an excellent spot to pick up pretty roses and in-season flowers to make an emergency bouquet or centerpiece.

PROBLEM: The floral tape is not holding the flowers together.

CAUSES: The floral tape was not "activated" by pulling it tightly or may be old and dried out.

SOLUTIONS: Make sure to activate the tape by pulling it tightly, or try new tape.

JEWELRY MAKING

PROBLEM: Crimping beads slide around on the necklace wire after they've been crimped.

CAUSES: The crimping beads were not crimped enough, or they may be too small for the tolerances of your tool.

SOLUTION: Make sure you're using a crimping tool to crimp the beads. Your crimping tool packaging will tell you what size crimping beads it is compatible with; make sure you're using the right size.

PAPER PROJECTS

PROBLEM: There are rough edges on the cardstock after cutting.

CAUSE: The blade on the paper cutter is dull.

SOLUTION: If your paper cutter has a removable and disposable blade, replace it. If you're using a guillotine-type cutter, see the manufacturer's recommendation for sharpening or replacing the blade.

PROBLEM: Printed graphics or images look pixilated or blurry.

CAUSE: The image is not print quality.

SOLUTIONS: Use the image at a smaller size or replace with a print-quality image of 180 dpi or greater.

PROBLEM: Cardstock won't feed through your printer.

CAUSE: Some printers won't accept thick papers or cardstocks; check the owner's manual for your printer's guidelines and paper-feed capabilities.

SOLUTIONS: Use either a thinner cardstock or a printer that can accommodate your cardstock.

PROBLEM: Printer ink smears on your cardstock.

CAUSE: The cardstock is likely a shimmer or gloss-coated paper and is not compatible with most printer inks.

SOLUTION: Use a non-shimmer or gloss-coated paper.

PROBLEM: The cardstock is crooked after cutting with a paper cutter.

CAUSES: The paper cutter is damaged or defective, or its arm, if it has a retractable one, is not fully extended. The paper is not aligned properly.

SOLUTION: Make sure the arm is fully extended and the paper is aligned properly. If that doesn't work, you will need to replace your paper cutter.

PROBLEM: When embroidering paper, the needle tears the paper.

CAUSES: The prepunched holes are too close together. The needle is too big or the embroidery floss is too thick for the holes. The cardstock is too thin to accommodate embroidery.

SOLUTIONS: Make sure to leave enough room between the holes to maneuver the needle and thread through. Use a thinner needle or floss or a thicker cardstock.

PROBLEM: Rubber-stamped image is blurry or smeared.

CAUSES: The ink is pigment-based and has not had ample time to dry. The rubber stamp was moved slightly when stamped onto the surface.

SOLUTIONS: If using a pigment-based ink, allow the image plenty of time to dry before moving on to any next steps. Do not rock or move your stamp while it's on the paper.

PROBLEM: Hole or paper punch doesn't penetrate cardstock or gets stuck.

CAUSES: The punch is clogged with paper or debris or is dull. The cardstock is too thick for the punch.

SOLUTIONS: Clear out all paper and debris from your punch. If your punch is dull, it will need to be replaced. If the cardstock is too thick, you will need to use either a stronger punch or thinner cardstock.

CREATIVE PAPERCLAY®

PROBLEM: The Paperclay cracks and crumbles when rolled out.

CAUSE: The Paperclay is too dry.

SOLUTION: Mist to rehydrate.

PROBLEM: The Paperclay is too sticky to handle.

CAUSE: The Paperclay is too wet.

SOLUTION: Allow it to dry a bit before handling.

PROBLEM: There are holes and bubbles in the rolled-out Paperclay.

CAUSE: The Paperclay was not properly kneaded to remove air pockets before being rolled out.

SOLUTION: Knead your Paperclay thoroughly before rolling it out again.

PRECIOUS METAL CLAY

PROBLEM: The precious metal clay (PMC) is dry and crumbly.

CAUSE: The PMC has dried out.

SOLUTION: Rehydrate the PMC by wrapping it in a slightly damp paper towel and putting it in a resealable bag overnight.

PROBLEM: The PMC is too sticky to handle.

CAUSE: The PMC has been oversaturated.

SOLUTION: Let it dry out a bit before handling.

PROBLEM: The PMC ring breaks apart while filing or sanding.

CAUSES: The clay was not dry enough (at the "leather-hard" stage) to handle, there were cracks or perforations that weakened it, or the user handled it too roughly. Gentle goes it before firing!

SOLUTION: You'll need to start the project over, but you can reuse this batch of clay. PMC can be rehydrated and reused at any stage before it's fired. Crumble the hardened clay, wrap it in a slightly damp paper towel, and put it in a resealable bag overnight.

PROBLEM: The PMC ring melts during firing.

CAUSE: The ring was heated for too long at too high of a temperature.

SOLUTION: Unfortunately, this is an instance where you'll have to start over. In your next firing, do be sure to keep the torch moving around the piece to help prevent hot spots and ensure the piece fires evenly.

CHAPTER ONE: *Sun & Sand*

WHO CAN RESIST the allure of a wedding by the water? Whether you're having a soiree on the beach, a lavish dockside affair, or an intimate day by a beautiful pond (or maybe you're a landlocked sea-loving couple), nautical-inspired crafts help set the mood for an unforgettable wedding. In this chapter, we will take common craft and seaside-themed items and combine them into lovely wedding elements.
Get started with a seashell-inspired paper clay ring bearer's cup that will work double duty post-wedding as a gorgeous jewelry dish. Next, send out a super-simple invitation that's embellished with a starfish. Then, how about creating a totally affordable and beautiful centerpiece with nautical rope? Round out your sand-and-sea theme by fashioning a stunning seashell boutonniere that your soon-to-be-hubby will be proud to wear. Finish it all off with adorable paper sailboat favors for your guests.

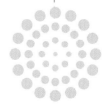

Paperclay Seashell Ring Dish

CRAFTY COMMITMENT

3 days

Though I typically love ring pillows, I love the idea of using an alternative mode of transportation for your precious wedding rings; something that can send your rings down the aisle in a fresh, new way and serve as a keepsake that you'll be able to display on your dresser at home after the big day. (Not like a pillow, which will likely be relegated to a hope chest, or worse, thrown away.) For you sea-inspired couples, you can create this darling ring dish. It's made of Creative Paperclay, hand stamped and painted to mimic the iridescence of beautiful seashells.

SOLO A-GO-GO

This is a perfect project to complete if you have short chunks of time to dedicate to crafting over a few days.

Paperclay is a nontoxic modeling material that feels similar to earthen clay but doesn't actually contain any clay. It's an "air-dry" clay, meaning you don't need an oven or any special equipment to solidify it. It can be found in most craft stores.

This project takes a bit of time to complete because the Paperclay and paints will need time to dry; allow 2 to 3 days to finish it up.

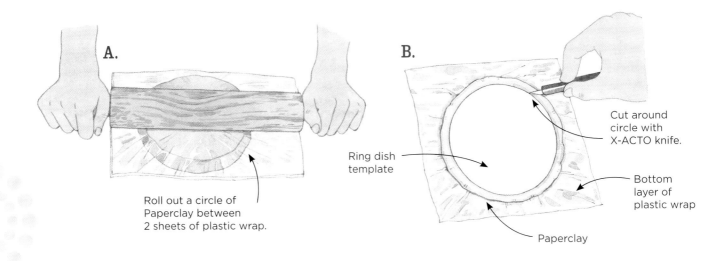

A.

Roll out a circle of Paperclay between 2 sheets of plastic wrap.

B.

Cut around circle with X-ACTO knife.

Ring dish template

Bottom layer of plastic wrap

Paperclay

SUPPLIES

- 8-oz. package of Creative Paperclay
- X-ACTO knife
- Plastic wrap
- Smooth acrylic or wood rolling pin
- Ring dish template
- Bamboo skewer or small rubber stamps
- Aluminum foil
- Paper towels
- Fine-grit sandpaper
- White acrylic craft paint
- Paint brush
- Clear matte polyurethane spray
- Black acrylic craft paint
- ¼-in.-wide ribbon, 12 in. long

DIRECTIONS

1. Remove the block of Paperclay from the packaging and cut it in half with the knife. Store the remaining Paperclay in an airtight container; otherwise it will dry out. Knead the Paperclay for a minute or two, until it is pliable. Shape it into a flat disk.

2. Tear off 2 pieces of plastic wrap, about 18 in. long. Place a piece of the plastic wrap on your work surface. Set the Paperclay disk in the center of the piece of plastic wrap, then cover it with the remaining piece.

3. With the rolling pin, roll the Paperclay into a circle, about ¼ in. in thickness. The result should be a smooth patty with no cracks or bumps **(drawing A)**.

4. Remove the top layer of plastic wrap and place the ring dish template on top of the Paperclay patty. While lightly holding the template in place, cut around it with the knife. Remove the excess clay and store it in your remainders container **(drawing B)**.

C.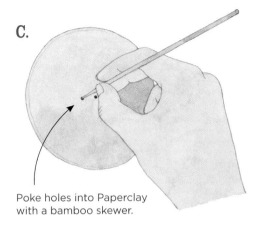

Poke holes into Paperclay with a bamboo skewer.

D.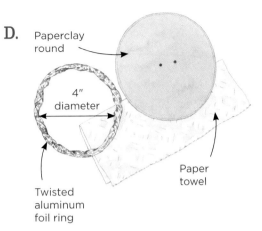

Paperclay round

4" diameter

Paper towel

Twisted aluminum foil ring

5. Dip your fingers in water and gently smooth away any marks, bumps, or imperfections. Use a light touch or you'll misshape your creation and will have to start over. (Paperclay is easy to rework: Just dampen it and knead it until it's pliable and smooth.)

6. Once you're satisfied with your seashell cutout, use the bamboo skewer or small rubber stamps to write or imprint your message into the surface of your Paperclay patty. Write a little larger than the final size you want the lettering to be; Paperclay will shrink a little as it dries. Now is the time to poke 2 holes into the center of the shell for the ribbon you'll be adding later **(drawing C)**.

7. Next, create a support for the ring dish. This will mold the sides into a bowl shape as the Paperclay dries. If you want a flat dish, skip this step. To make the support, twist a 12-in. length of aluminum foil into a rope-like shape. Curl it around into a small circle, about 4 in. in diameter and ½ in. high. Cover the circle with a paper towel or two so that the aluminum foil doesn't imprint on the clay. Gently lift the Paperclay patty and place in into the foil circle. The weight of the Paperclay will pull the center down to

continued on p. 16

create a bowl shape **(drawing D)**. Allow the Paperclay to dry overnight or however long it needs to become fully dry.

8. Using the fine-grit sandpaper, gently smooth out any bumps or imperfections. Wipe the dust away with a paper towel or soft cloth.

9. Once the Paperclay is dry and baby-bottom smooth, paint it white. Let it dry completely, at least 24 hours. When you add wet paint to the Paperclay, the moisture will be absorbed into it,

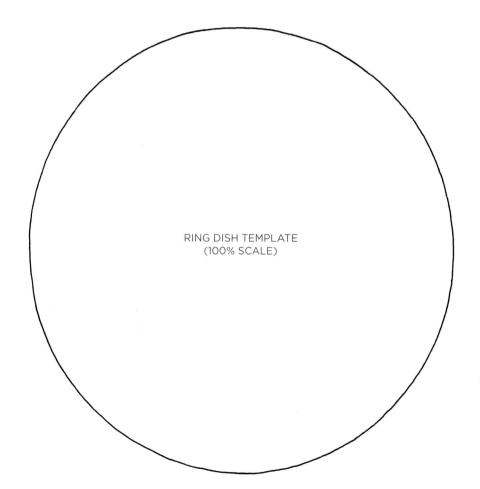

RING DISH TEMPLATE
(100% SCALE)

so you'll need to account for extra drying time beyond just the paint surface.

10. Phew! You're almost finished. Take your beautiful ring holder outside and give it a light, even coat of polyurethane. Allow it to completely dry.

11. Next, squirt a small dollop of black paint onto the writing on the shell. Using a paper towel, push the paint into the cracks and crevices of the writing, then wipe away the remaining paint. The black paint will sink into the writing, making it really stand out.

12. From the bottom of the dish, thread the ribbon into the holes. Tie your rings into a neat little bow and you're ready to go!

tips & hints

- *Paperclay is wonderfully easy to work with, but it does need to be kept moist while you work with it. Keep a spray bottle or bowl of water close by to give the clay a bit of a mist while you're working. Just don't soak it.*

- *The Paperclay will take on any imperfections or bumps from the rolling pin, your fingers, or the work surface. Do make sure your surfaces are as smooth as possible.*

- *Paperclay can be imprinted by nearly anything. Try a rubber stamp like I did for the swirl detail in this project, lace fabric, leaves, real seashells, thumbprints, or vintage cookie molds.*

Price Breakdown

YOUR COST

8 oz. of Creative Paperclay	$6.00
Sandpaper	$2.00
2 bottles of acrylic paint	$2.00
Can of polyurethane	$6.00
Ribbon	$3.00
TOTAL	**$19.00**

STORE COST
Custom ring bearer vessels cost upward of $45.00 from specialty designers.

Please join us in celebration of love and
laughter as

Michelle Elena Williams
and
Michael Johnson Galeazzi

Join their hands in marriage

Saturday, June 15th, 2012
5 o'clock in the afternoon
Hoby Beach, Plettenberg Bay

Sea-and-Sand Invitation

So, if you're on a budget and—if you're like more than one-third of my brides—you consider yourself in that often overlooked micro-budget category, finding invitations that can be made for less than 70 cents each is like the Holy Grail of DIY projects. Luckily for you, my penny-pinching princess, your seaside wedding perfectly lends itself to budget-friendly projects. The beauty and bounty of the sea is the ideal backdrop and theme for a stunning wedding.

As a general rule, my go-to project on the cheap is stationery. Cardstock is abundant and inexpensive. Most everyone has access to Microsoft® Word, a printer, and a paper cutter. The real expense for stationery comes from the embellishments and the time you put into it.

For my beach-themed couples, I've created this simple layered invitation that incorporates inexpensive starfish. It's a nice way to set the tone for a beautiful and classic beach soiree for your guests without breaking the bank. Whether you're on a strict budget or are looking for a standout invite, this is a great project for you!

CRAFTY COMMITMENT

5 to 10 minutes per invitation

WITH A LITTLE HELP FROM MY FRIENDS

This is an easy project for your willing but not-so-crafty helpers. Divide up the cutting, punching, starfish gluing, and layering duties among your crew members to create a speedy assembly line.

SUPPLIES

- White cardstock,
  8½ in. by 11 in.

- Moss green cardstock,
  8½ in. by 11 in.

- Kraft cardstock,
  8½ in. by 11 in.

- Paper cutter

- Scalloped circle paper
  punch, 1 in. diameter

- Hot glue gun and glue

- Small dried starfish,
  available through online
  retailers (see Resources,
  page 216) in bulk

- Computer with
  Microsoft Word

- Printer

- Double-sided tape

DIRECTIONS

1. To make your crafting time more efficient, I recommend precutting your cardstock to its finished dimensions before you start. For this invitation, the white cardstock should be cut to 4¼ in. by 4¼ in. The green cardstock should be cut to 4½ in. by 4½ in., and, finally, the kraft cardstock to 5 in. by 5 in.

2. The next step is to create the star-in-circle embellishments. From a sheet of kraft cardstock, punch several scalloped circles with your paper punch. Using the hot glue gun, apply a tiny bit of hot glue to the back of a starfish. Quickly press it, glue side down, in the center of one of the punched circles. Set them aside for the final assembly.

3. Now it's time to create the printed portion of the template. Open Microsoft Word and create a new document.

4. From the Page Setup menu, select "Custom Page Size" from the "Settings" options. Set the custom page size for "4.25" wide by "4.25" high. Click "OK."

5. Set the margin spacing to "0.25" for the left and right margins. For the top and bottom, set the margin spacing to "0.25" as a starting point for your margins. Depending on the size of your shells and the length of your wording, you'll need to adjust the top margin to fit all of the embellishments and information.

6. This step is where you get to showcase your creativity! Using your favorite fonts and best wording skills, enter the invitation information. Save and print the invitation document onto the 4¼-in. by 4¼-in. white cardstock **(photo A)**.

7. Now it's time to assemble these beauties! On the back of one of the printed invitation pieces, apply double-sided tape. Turn it over and adhere this piece of cardstock to one of the green 4½-in. by

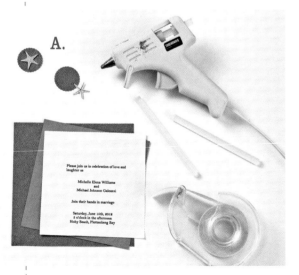

A.

4$\frac{1}{2}$-in. pieces of cardstock, centering it from top to bottom and from side to side. On the back of this stack, apply double-sided tape and adhere it to the front of the kraft cardstock piece. You're almost done!

8. To finish off the invitation, apply double-sided tape to the back of the starfish circle embellishment and adhere it to the front of the invitation part of the stack, centering it from side to side.

tips & hints

- *Cardstock is quite inexpensive, making this one of the least expensive projects in the book.*

- *Cardstock is available in an endless rainbow of hues and shades. Nearly every couple will be able to find the perfect combination of colors to suit their individual style.*

- *Play around with different font styles and sizes to add visual interest to your invitation. Visit www.dafont.com, one of the best sources for free, quality fonts.*

- *Starfish come in a wide array of sizes from bulk seashell providers. I like $\frac{1}{2}$-in. starfish for the scale of this project. You can add larger or even different species of shells.*

- *Square invitations often cost more to send than rectangular ones. If you're sending 100 invitations, it can add up quickly! Take a finished invite down to your local post office and let them advise you on how much postage your invite will need. Do account for the extra postage in your budget.*

FIT YOUR STYLE

Garden-wedding couples can adapt this invitation by substituting dried flowers or leaves for the starfish. For a winter wedding, use glittered paper snowflakes.

Price Breakdown

YOUR COST

Cardstock for 50 invitations	**$25.00**
Hot glue	**$1.00**
Tape	**$0.10**
Starfish	**$8.75**

TOTAL	**$34.85**
	for 50 invites or
	$0.69 each

STORE COST

Custom-designed invitations with real starfish from professional stationers cost **$4.75** each.

Rope-Wrapped Centerpiece

Judging from the oodles of e-mail that I receive every month, centerpieces are among the most sought-after and agonized-over projects by do-it-yourselfers. It's no wonder; a simple centerpiece from a high-end designer can cost hundreds of dollars, which is out of the financial comfort zone of most couples.

When I brainstorm centerpiece ideas, my goal is to keep the price around $50 per table. As you've probably guessed, that's quite a task!

For nautical-themed weddings, I wanted to pull together something that had a seaside feel but was subtle enough to use with nearly any outdoor theme. The answer was rope. Not only does every boater or sailor rely heavily on rope, but many types are also rather lovely and perfect for decorative purposes. And it's cheap!

This rope-wrapped vase holds a beautiful arrangement of hydrangea and godetia, two flowers that are abundant and reasonably priced year-round. Even better, it's quick and easy to assemble, which means you can do it solo or with a friend in an afternoon. Grab your glue gun and get wrapping!

CRAFTY COMMITMENT

10 to 15 minutes for the vase; 20 minutes more for the arrangement

WITH A LITTLE HELP FROM MY FRIENDS

Grab some lemonade and head outside for some relaxing craft time on the patio when you're creating the vases. On the big day, hand off the floral arranging to a trusted friend or two while you're off being a beautiful bride.

SUPPLIES

- Glass cylinder vase, 12 in. tall by 5 in. in diameter
- Glass cleaner and paper towels
- Glue gun and glue sticks
- $3/8$-in.-diameter sisal rope, one 50-ft. roll (enough for 1 centerpiece with 3 vases), available at most hardware stores
- Floral shears
- 5 heads of blue and white hydrangea
- 1 dozen godetia flowers

DIRECTIONS

1. Begin this super-easy project by cleaning the outside of the vase with glass cleaner. Dry the vase with paper towels or let air-dry.

2. While your vase is drying, plug in your glue gun so that the glue can start liquefying.

3. Place a dollop of glue on the vase, near the bottom edge. Immediately place the end of the rope into the glue, parallel to the bottom. Be very careful! Hot glue is indeed very hot and can cause severe burning. Hold the rope in place for a few seconds to ensure that it adheres to the glass.

4. Finish wrapping the rope tightly around the vase, adding a dollop of glue every 1 to 2 turns around the glass **(photo A)**.

5. Cut the rope with your floral shears when the vase is completely wrapped and secure the end with one last dollop of glue. The glue should hold the end in place and prevent the cut rope from fraying.

A.

FIT YOUR STYLE

Winter wedding and fairy-tale wedding couples can make this upscale by using garlands of faux crystals, found at big box craft stores, in place of rope. Having a modern wedding? Use metallic cording from fabric shops for something with a bit of an industrial feel.

6. Let the vase cool completely (the glass will retain heat from the hot glue for a while) before filling it with water.

7. Trim the stems of your flowers to fit the height of the vase.

8. To finish off the centerpieces, simply add water to the vase and insert your flowers.

tips & hints

- *Plain, smooth vases are easily found in most craft stores and are often on sale.*

- *Check out dollar discount stores for incredibly inexpensive vases to save some cash.*

- *If you're looking for something a bit quirky, mismatched vases can be found at secondhand stores for next to nothing.*

- *If you're lucky enough to have an IKEA® nearby, do check out their selection of inexpensive vases.*

- *Who says you need a glass vase? Tin cans, old pottery, plastic 2-liter bottles, and clay pots can also be roped up.*

- *Sisal rope can be dyed to nearly any color you want.*

- *The downside of sisal is that it sheds like crazy. You may want to do the wrapping outside.*

- *Nylon rope and decorative cording from fabric stores work great for this project, but they are a bit more expensive.*

Price Breakdown

YOUR COST

Vase	**$5.00**
Rope	**$8.50**
Godetia	**$25.00**
Hydrangea	**$10.00**
Hot glue	**$4.00**

TOTAL

	$52.50

STORE COST

Florists will charge anywhere from **$60** to **$80** for a similar centerpiece.

Seashell Boutonniere

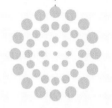

My friends Jamie and Clint were frustrated when planning their coastal Maryland wedding. They were going for a casual, small-town, beach theme. Much of the wedding inspiration available to them at the time was heavily tropical-influenced or was more suited for the California coast than the Atlantic coast.

For Clint's boutonniere, I wanted to create something that was far from tropical but that still captured a by-the-sea vibe. Combining delicate greenery with a pure white flower and a handsome seashell fit the order. My friends were thrilled with the boutonniere and how smashing it looked with Clint's linen suit on their wedding day.

The white and green foliage used in this boutonniere is called Snow on the Mountain or, botanically, *Euphorbia marginata*. Ironically, it grows wild on the plains of Colorado, but it's available through specialty retailers online or you may order through your local florist. Its availability is May through September. Lovely and fragrant, the white flower is tuberose. It can be found at numerous online flower shops and is available year-round. Your flowers should be purchased (or scheduled for delivery) 3 days before your wedding.

CRAFTY COMMITMENT

10 to 15 minutes

WITH A LITTLE HELP FROM MY FRIENDS

While this is a quick and easy project, it must be done on the day of the wedding. Enlist the help of a trusted pal to carry out the assembly tasks so you can relax and enjoy your big day.

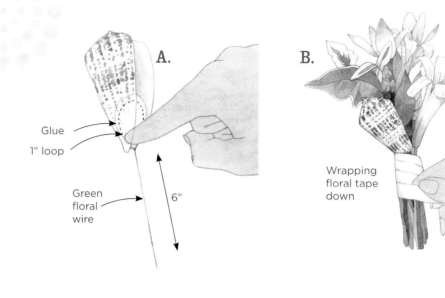

A.

Glue

1" loop

Green
floral
wire

6"

B.

Wrapping
floral tape
down

SUPPLIES

- Hot glue gun and glue
- Green floral wire
- Wire cutters
- 1 medium seashell, about $2\frac{1}{2}$ in. tall
- 1 bunch Snow on the Mountain greenery
- 1 stem of tuberose
- Floral tape
- Floral shears
- White ribbon
- Scissors
- Boutonniere pins

DIRECTIONS

1. Kick off this easy-to-assemble craft by creating a stem for your seashell. Plug in and heat up your glue gun. Cut about a 6-in. piece of wire from the spool. When the glue is ready, turn the shell over to expose its open side. Place a generous pool of glue inside the opening, near the bottom of the shell, and firmly press one end of the wire into it. Hold the wire in place for a few seconds, until the glue starts to cool and can support the wire on its own **(drawing A)**.

2. Next, bring together a sprig from the bunch of Snow on the Mountain and a stem of tuberose. Remove any excess leaves to scale the boutonniere to the wearer; you want to create a nice, compact arrangement.

3. While still holding your flowers and foliage, add in the wired shell. Use floral tape to secure all of the pieces in place, and wrap floral tape down the stems in a spiral to secure them together, wrapping until about $\frac{3}{4}$ in. is covered.

4. Trim away the excess stem and wire. Continue to wrap floral tape around the bunch, about 3 in. down, then wrap the tape back up toward the flower head **(drawing B)**.

5. To finish the boutonniere, trim the wired and wrapped stem so the total length is about 1½ in. Wrap a length of ribbon around the stem, securing it in place with boutonniere pins. Great job!

tips & hints

- *Due to their delicate nature, flowers must be stored in water and in a cool place. Refrigerators are often too cold. A spare bedroom or bathroom or even a cellar is usually your best bet.*

- *Tuberoses are highly fragrant flowers. If your groom or groomsmen have sensitivity to fragrance, this is not the flower to use! Recommended substitutions are stephanotis, white Alstroemeria, small spray roses, or an orchid.*

- *Ordering flowers through your local florists can often be less expensive than ordering from online flower providers, but not always. Ask your florist for pricing before you order, and be sure to ask if shipping is included.*

- *To perk things up a bit, use a contrasting ribbon color, such as coral. It looks fab against the green and white foliage and highlights the beautiful shell colors.*

- *This is a project that's best done the day of the wedding. Please hand this off to a trusted helper, with complete instructions.*

FIT YOUR STYLE

Modern-themed wedding couples can take advantage of this lovely project by using dried seed pods or something quirky like bright clusters of buttons in lieu of seashells.

Price Breakdown

YOUR COST

Hot glue	$4.00
Floral wire	$2.00
Seashells	$4.00
Snow on the Mountain	$11.00
Tuberose	$6.50
Floral tape	$3.00
Ribbon	$1.00
Pins	$2.00

TOTAL

$33.50
for 4 to 6 boutonnieres

STORE COST

Florists charge upward of **$20** for a single simple boutonniere.

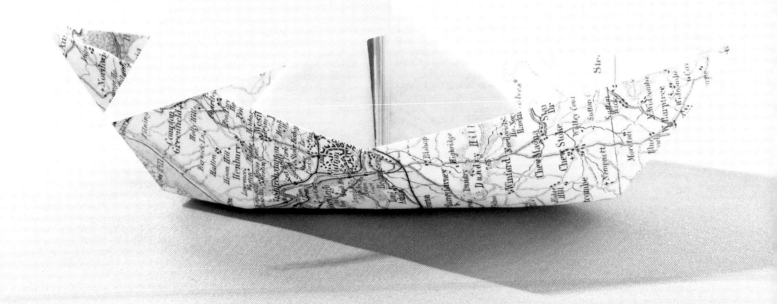

Paper Boat Favor Container

I have a lifelong obsession with boats. Not only do I have a degree in naval architecture, but I'm also a longtime sailor and a former sail maker. My preoccupation with all things nautical can be traced to my earliest days of crafting, when I made paper boats to sail in our neighborhood park's fountain. I spent countless hours as a kid making precious paper armadas, only to see them waterlogged and sent to a watery grave within an afternoon.

I recently resurrected my origami skills to combine my two loves—crafting and boats—in an effort to help you create some nautical goodness for your wedding. These adorable paper boats are designed not for setting sail on the open water but to hold small treats for your guests such as candy or caramel corn.

Though these are fairly easy to make, they are a bit time-consuming, especially when doing 100 or more of them. Do gather together friends and family for a paper-folding party to help make light work of such a huge project.

CRAFTY COMMITMENT

15 to 20 minutes per favor

WITH A LITTLE HELP FROM MY FRIENDS

Building a paper armada takes a whole crew of helpers. Grab your best mates for an afternoon of boat-building fun. Set up stations for folding, stamping, and assembly to make the most of your crafting time together.

A.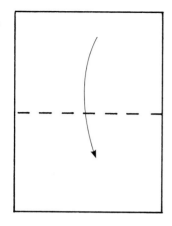

B.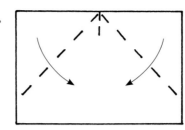

C.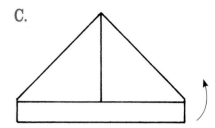

SUPPLIES

- Nautical maps, cut to 8½ in. by 11 in.
- Sail template
- Off-white cardstock, 12 in. by 12 in.
- X-ACTO knife or craft shears
- Bamboo skewers
- Double-sided tape
- Pennant template
- Ink pad
- Small alphabet rubber stamp set
- Clear tape

DIRECTIONS FOR FOLDING THE BOATS

1. Fold an 8½-in. by 11-in. map in half along its width, with the folded edge away from you **(drawing A)**.

2. Fold the two top corners in so they meet at the middle and form a triangle. There will be about an inch left over on the bottom; this leaves an open flap on each side of the triangle **(drawing B)**.

3. Fold the front flap up to the front, then fold the back flap up to the back **(drawing C)**.

4. Take hold of the left and right corners and push them together so they lie flat against each other **(drawing D)**. As you push them together, pull apart the center front and back of the triangle. You should now have a diamond shape **(drawing E)**.

5. Still with me? Now fold the bottom corners on the front and back of the diamond to meet at the top corner. This creates an open-bottomed triangle **(drawing E)**.

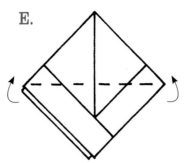

E.

F.

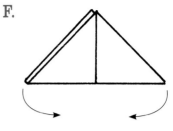

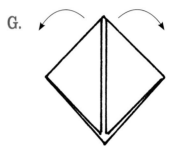

G.

H.

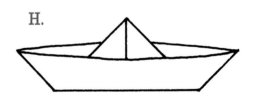

6. Pull the triangle open, flattening the opposite sides against each other as you marvelously did in step 4 **(drawing F)**.

7. Now this is where the boat takes shape. Pull the top layer out on both sides (left and right). It looks like the hull of a boat, right **(drawings G and H)**? After a few of these, you'll be able to do them in your sleep in no time.

DIRECTIONS FOR DECORATING THE BOATS

1. Copy the sail template onto a piece of heavy cardstock. Cut the sail shape out and use it to trace onto the cardstock you've set aside for the sail. You should be able to get a couple of sails out of each sheet of cardstock. Cut out the sail shapes from the cardstock using the X-ACTO knife.

2. Cut bamboo skewers to 6 in. tall. Using double-sided tape, attach the sails to the skewers, leaving 1 in. at the top for the pennant.

3. Copy the pennant template onto heavy cardstock. Cut the pennant shape out and use it to trace onto the cardstock you've set aside for the pennant. Cut out the pennant shapes and fold them in half.

continued on p. 34

4. Ink up your rubber stamp letters to spell "love" and press firmly onto one side of the folded pennant. Set each pennant aside to dry.

5. Once your pennants are stamped and dry, apply a line of double-sided tape on the inside. Place the pennant near the top of the skewer and fold over, sealing the two pennant sides together around the skewer.

6. Now attach the skewer and sail combination to the inside of the boat with a strip of clear tape.

7. Fill the boats with your favorite treats. Life Savers®, anyone?

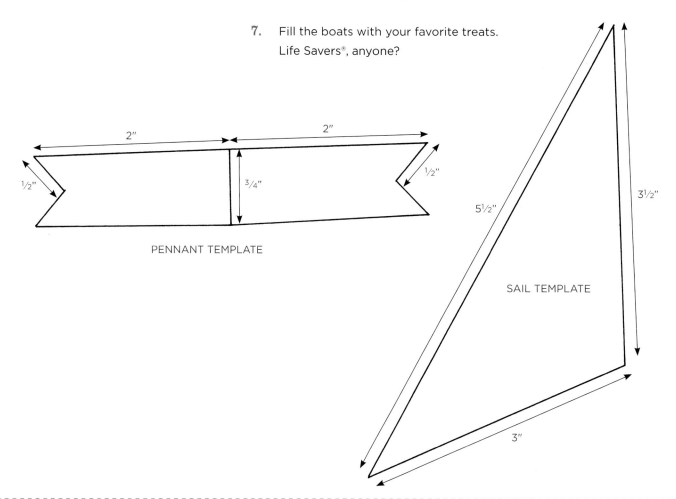

PENNANT TEMPLATE

SAIL TEMPLATE

tips & hints

- *If you're not lucky enough to stumble into a cache of vintage nautical charts, contemporary ones are available for download online. Do make sure the ones you grab are print-quality, at least 300 dpi.*

- *Should you print your own charts, do print on both sides of the paper, and make sure that your image is borderless (usually a setting in your printer menu). Double-sided copies are easily done at the major copy shops—and probably cheaper than using up your ink at home.*

- *Any pattern or motif can be used for the boats. Solid colors work well in the nautical theme, as do celestial maps, semaphore flags, any kind of map, or pages from Horatio Hornblower novels.*

- *The pennant can say anything you want. If "love" is too pedestrian for your tastes, go for your newlywed monogram. How about writing your guests' names in a beautiful script? Cute nautical sayings like "Ahoy!" are fun, too.*

Price Breakdown

YOUR COST

Nautical map	**free**
Paper to print nautical maps, 25 sheets	$0.10
Cardstock, 25 sheets	$8.75
Skewers	$1.00
Tape	$4.00

TOTAL $13.85
for 25 boat containers or **$0.55** each

STORE COST

Non-embellished paper boat favor holders cost upward of **$2.00** per favor from specialty vendors.

CHAPTER TWO: *Fairy-Tale Wedding*

DREAMS DO COME true, especially for you, my hopelessly romantic friend. If you consider yourself a princess bride marrying her charming prince, let this fairy-tale wedding chapter inspire you to incorporate luxury and fantasy into an affordable wedding day that's fit for a royal couple like you!

Set the tone of your wedding with an ultra-luxe invitation made of beautiful satin with a beaded overlay. Help your guests find their tables with blinged-out crystal-accented table numbers. Get your flower girls in on the princess-y fun with their own fairy wings and tutus. Don't forget about your maids! Add a touch of glamour to their gowns with a simple-to-make but oh-so-pretty sash. The final touch to your all-out-gorgeous affair? A bejeweled bouquet wrap that turns even the simplest bouquet into an extraordinary accessory.

Accordion-Fold Invitation

Every great love has a romantic story behind it. Why not create your own book of fairy tales as you invite your guests to your once-in-a-lifetime wedding? This accordion-fold booklet-style invitation features four panels that allow you to share your story while at the same time conveying all of the important wedding-related information. Adorned with a satin and beaded tulle cover, it combines romance and fantasy in one drop-dead-gorgeous package.

The high price of beauty for this project is that it's labor-intensive. Between creating the covers, cutting, printing, and assembling, each invitation takes 30 to 45 minutes to complete. You're worth the effort, of course; just allow yourself plenty of time to complete your masterpieces. A stressful beginning isn't the best way to start your happily-ever-after!

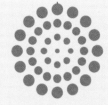

CRAFTY COMMITMENT

30 to 45 minutes per invitation

WITH A LITTLE HELP FROM MY FRIENDS

Labor-intensive projects like this are best done with helping hands. Gather your maids-in-waiting for a weekend of crafty goodness. (Bribes of good food, chick flicks, and cocktails always help boost the volunteer pool.) For maximum efficiency, set up a station for cutting fabric, ribbon, and paper; another for creating the covers; one for inserts; and another for the final assembly.

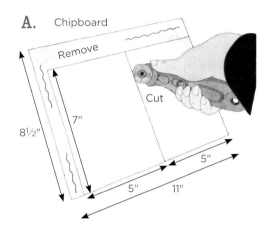

A. Chipboard

Remove

Cut

8½"

7"

5"

5"

11"

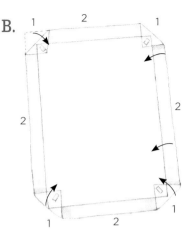

B.

1

2

1

1

2

2

2

1

1

2

1

1. Fold fabric corners inward; secure with double-sided tape.

2. Fold in sides of fabric toward the middle of chipboard; secure with double-sided tape.

SUPPLIES

- 1 sheet of chipboard, 8½ in. by 11 in., available at craft and scrapbook stores
- Rotary cutter or paper cutter
- Ruler
- Satin fabric in white, 1 yd.
- Beaded tulle, 1 yd.
- Scissors
- Red-lined double-sided tape, available at most craft stores in the adhesive aisle
- 2 sheets of pink cardstock, 8½ in. by 11 in.
- Bone folder
- Computer with Microsoft Word
- Printer
- 2 sheets of white cardstock, 8½ in. by 11 in.
- 1-in.-wide ribbon in pink, 12 in. long

DIRECTIONS

1. Cut the chipboard sheet into two 5-in. by 7-in. pieces using the rotary cutter and ruler or a heavy-duty paper cutter **(drawing A)**.

2. From both the satin and beaded tulle, cut two 6-in. by 8-in. pieces. You'll end up with a front piece and a back piece for the top and bottom covers of the invitation.

3. Place a chipboard piece onto the center of one of the white satin pieces of fabric. If your chipboard has a brown side and a white side, make sure the white side is facing the white fabric. You wouldn't want the dark brown showing through on your invitation cover.

4. Fold the corners of the fabric inward, diagonally, toward the center.

5. Apply a small strip of double-sided tape on the underside of the corner to hold it in place. Do this for all 4 corners, making sure the fabric is taut and wrinkle-free. Fold in the sides of the fabric toward the middle of the chipboard. Again, use a strip of double-sided tape to adhere the fabric **(drawing B)**.

6. Now place the satin-covered chipboard onto the center of the beaded tulle. Repeat steps 4 and 5 **(photo A)**. Set your covers aside and move on to creating the accordion. The accordion will serve as the base for you to attach individual panels with your wedding information in a later step.

7. Cut two pieces of pink cardstock to 7 in. tall by 10½ in. wide.

8. With a bone folder and ruler, score the cardstock at the measurements shown in **drawing C**.

9. Using double-sided tape, adhere one of the two ½-in. pieces on top of the other. This creates a single piece of cardstock that's 7 in. tall and 20 in. wide.

10. Let's assemble the book! Apply a liberal amount of tape on the back side of the left-most 5-in. by 7-in. panel of the pink cardstock. Align the cardstock on the back (inner) side of the front cover of the invitation. Press it firmly in place, burnishing it with the bone folder to make sure it's permanently stuck in place.

continued on p. 42

FIT YOUR STYLE

Garden-wedding couples can substitute the tulle and satin with a cute gingham or lightweight burlap.

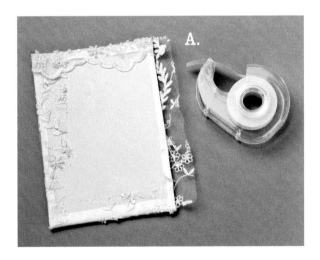

A.

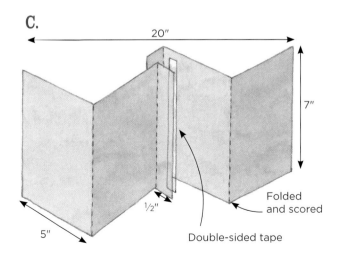

C.

20"

7"

½"

5"

Double-sided tape

Folded and scored

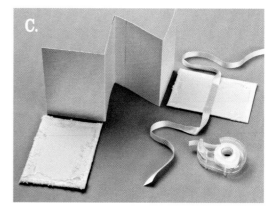

Price Breakdown

YOUR COST

Chipboard for 12 invitations	**$8.00**
Fabric	**$20.00**
Tape	**$6.00**
Cardstock	**$8.50**
Ribbon	**$2.00**

TOTAL	**$44.50**
	for 12 invites
	or **$3.70** each

STORE COST

High-end stationers charge upward of **$20** each for custom, fabric-covered booklet invitations.

11. Fold the 12-in.-long piece of ribbon in half. At the fold, tape it down onto the back (inner) side of the back cover of the invitation, centering it from side to side and top to bottom **(photo B)**.

12. Apply a liberal amount of tape on the right-most 5-in. by 7-in. panel of pink cardstock. Align the back cover panel and stick it down. You'll now have a lovely fabric-covered accordion-fold book that's empty inside **(photo C)**. Let's move on to creating the invitation pieces.

13. Open Microsoft Word and create a new document.

14. From the Page Setup menu, select "Custom Page Size" from the "Settings" options. Set the custom page size for "5" wide by "7" high. Click "OK."

15. Set the margin spacing to "0.25" for the left and right margins. For the top and bottom, set the margin spacing to "0.25."

16. Using your favorite fonts, enter the invitation information, dedicating each page to a different section. I love the idea of opening to a short welcome page that tells a little bit about the bride and groom. The second page is perfect for displaying the

wedding invitation. The third page is suited to travel information or other wedding-related events. The final page could be RSVP instructions or some final words from the couple. Save and print the invitation documents onto white cardstock that's been cut to 5 in. by 7 in.

17. On the back of each invitation page, apply double-sided tape. Line the pages up to their corresponding spots on the inner pink panels of the accordion fold and adhere them together.

18. Close the book and bring the ends of the ribbon to the front and tie a pretty bow. Trim off any excess ribbon. You're ready to send what are undoubtedly some of the most beautiful invitations ever created. You rock, crafty princess!

tips & hints

- I've used two layers of fabric here to create the feel of an ornate bridal gown. You may use whatever fabric or combination of fabric you like. Continuing with a fairy-tale theme, rich brocades, sumptuous silks, and luxurious taffetas would all work well.

- If you're having trouble finding chipboard, use cereal boxes! They're about the right thickness. Do make sure to cover the packaging design well with your cardstock and fabric. A Cheerios™ box doesn't instill a sense of royalty or romance when peeking through your invitation materials. Buzzkill!

- This project is perfect for groups of people to tackle. Put your maids to work, but please, don't play the part of the evil stepsister. Keep workdays short and treat your helpers to yummy snacks or drinks at the end of their shift.

- Do make sure your chipboard and cardboard cuts are as straight as possible. If they're even a little crooked, it can throw off the alignment of the pages. Use a new, sharp blade in your paper cutter or rotary cutter; it helps.

- If you end up with a fraying fabric, seek out liquid fray-stoppers at fabric stores. Dab a bit on the edges of your fabric and it'll help prevent further fraying. Another trick is to spray your fabric with liquid starch and iron it. The starch helps bind the fabric's fibers together so that they don't unravel easily.

- The best way to send these is inside a stationery box. Paper Source and Paper Mart both have very nice boxes that fit this invitation perfectly. Beware: These will be expensive to ship!

- Sign up for your local big box fabric store's newsletter. Many offer discount coupons and presales for their subscribers.

Crystal-Accented Table Number

You want grand glam on a modest budget. There's nothing wrong with that! The key to bringing a bit of luxury to your wedding is to select a few choice elements to embellish with luxurious materials. Little details go a long way and allow you to make small splurges that have maximum impact.

For an ultra-chic table, I love taking something common and plain—like this table number—and giving it a blinged-out makeover. By adding some inexpensive scrapbook paper and sparkly rhinestones, it goes from bland to grand in a few easy (and cheap) steps.

CRAFTY COMMITMENT

3 hours

WITH A LITTLE HELP FROM MY FRIENDS

Make quick work of a big project with the helping hands of your friends and family. Put someone on cutting duty and the rest on assembly and embellishment. Treat everyone to yummy cocktails when it's all done.

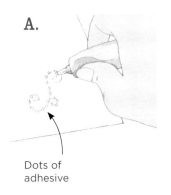

A.

Dots of
adhesive

B.

Set rhinestones
onto glue.

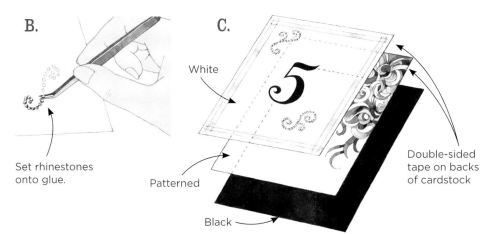

C.

White

Patterned

Black

Double-sided
tape on backs
of cardstock

SUPPLIES

- Computer with Microsoft Word

- Printer

- White cardstock, cut to 4 in. by 6 in.

- Pencil

- Rhinestone adhesive

- Tweezers

- 4-mm to 6-mm clear flat-back rhinestones, about 80 pieces per table number, depending on your design

- Double-sided tape

- Patterned paper, cut to 4½ in. by 6½ in.

- Black cardstock, cut to 5 in. by 7 in.

- Hole punch

- ¼-in.-wide ribbon, 12 in. long

DIRECTIONS

1. To set up your table numbers for printing, open Microsoft Word and create a new document. From the Page Setup menu, select "Custom Page Size" from the "Settings" options. Set the custom page size for "4" wide by "6." Click "OK." Set the margin spacing to "0.25" for the left and right margins. For the top, set the margin spacing to "0.25." For the bottom, set the spacing to "0.50."

2. Enter your table number in a pretty font. Center it, top to bottom and left to right, on the page. Save the document and print it onto the precut white cardstock.

3. With a pencil, lightly draw a design on the cardstock where you'd like to add your rhinestone bling. Do make sure the design is open and wide enough for the rhinestones to fit without overcrowding or distorting your design.

4. Trace the design with rhinestone adhesive, using small dots along the pencil lines you created **(drawing A)**.

5. With tweezers, pick up a rhinestone and gently set it onto the glue. Press down to secure it in place. Move on to the next, alternating sizes **(drawing B)**. Let the glue dry according to the manufacturer's recommendations.

6. Now it's time to assemble the table numbers. Add strips of double-sided tape to the back of the white cardstock piece. Center it over a piece of the patterned paper and press down to secure it in place. Next, add double-sided tape to the back of the patterned paper stack and center it over a piece of black cardstock. Press it firmly in place **(drawing C)**.

7. The final step is to punch a hole near the top of the table number with a hole punch, centered about ½ in. from the top edge. Thread a length of ribbon through and tie to your flower arrangement.

FIT YOUR STYLE

Modern couples can adapt this by using a decorative paper in a simple geometric print with metal brads (found at craft stores). Having a garden wedding? Try using a cute floral paper and adding birdseed embellishments.

tips & hints

- Cardstocks and papers come in thousands of colors and patterns. The best spots for finding beautiful and even trendy designs are at scrapbook and art stores.

- Rhinestones come in all colors of the rainbow. When buying in bulk, it's best to search the Internet for the best pricing.

- If swirls aren't your thing, how about a rhinestone monogram? Or blinging out the number itself?

- Rhinestones look great when they're paired on a table with candlelight. The sparkle and shine is simply gorgeous.

- There are plastic rhinestones on the market, and yes, they are considerably cheaper than crystal or glass versions. Unfortunately, they're not as pretty and lose a lot of the "wow" factor that the real deal gives.

Price Breakdown

YOUR COST

Cardstock	$10.00
Adhesive	$4.00
Rhinestones	$14.00
Double-sided tape	$4.00
Patterned paper	$11.00
Ribbon	$3.00

TOTAL $46.00
for 20 table numbers or
$2.30 each

STORE COST

Custom-designed table numbers from online vendors start at around **$4.00** each and go up from there.

Fairy-Tale Flower Girl Costume

What fairy-tale wedding would be complete without fairies? Certainly not yours! Every princess bride needs a fairy sidekick to scatter petals down the aisle and add that "Awwwww, isn't she adorable?" factor that helps make a wedding a cherished family affair. With this ultra-pretty fairy costume, your flower girl can play princess right alongside you on your most magical of days.

Patience will definitely be a virtue when creating the fairy wings. Wrangling the wire into shape can be a challenge and will very likely be what you spend the most time on in the process. Allow plenty of production time for the wings, at least 3 to 4 hours. The good news is that the tutu is almost ridiculously easy to complete and takes about an hour of your time. The materials for this entire costume are easily found at your local fabric and hardware stores.

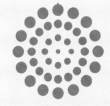

CRAFTY COMMITMENT

5 hours

SOLO A-GO-GO

This is a great project to do while watching your favorite guilty-pleasure TV show. Bonus points if it involves vampires.

SUPPLIES

Wing Supplies

- 16-gauge craft wire
- Wire cutters
- Duct tape
- Organza fabric with iridescent or glittered swirls, 2 yd.
- Fabric marker
- Scissors
- Needle and thread to match the organza fabric
- 1-in.-wide ribbon to coordinate with the ensemble's colors, 1 yd.
- Hot glue gun and glue
- 1 large silk flower

Tutu Supplies

- Measuring tape
- 1-in.-wide elastic
- Needle and thread
- Scissors or rotary cutter
- 6-in.-wide tulle in the color(s) of your choice, three 25-yd. rolls

DIRECTIONS FOR FAIRY WINGS

1. To get started, cut a 6-ft. length of wire for the upper wings. Gently bend the wire to bring the two ends together with about an inch overlap. Duct tape the ends together, making sure to cover the cut ends of the wire with tape so that they don't poke your precious princess. You should now have a soft oval-shaped wire frame **(drawing A)**.

2. Bring the top and bottom centers of your wire together to form a figure-8 shape. Again, whip out your trusty duct tape and secure the center section together, creating about a 2 in. wide flat area in the middle. Set your top wings aside and create the bottom set **(drawing B)**.

3. Cut a 4-ft. length of wire and repeat steps 1 and 2.

4. Now it's time to give the wings some shape. The great thing about wings is that they come in all shapes and sizes, so whatever you design, it is going to be perfect. Use your fingers to bend one side of the wire frame into your wing shape. I find it's easiest to shape one wing and then gently fold the frame in half so that you can use the finished side as a template for the other. It helps keep them symmetrical. Repeat this step for the bottom wings **(drawing C)**.

FIT YOUR STYLE

Winter wedding couples can be guided down the aisle by a beauty all in winter white just by changing the color of the fabrics used.

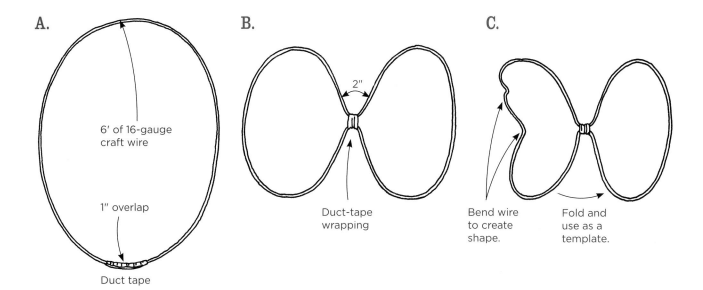

A. 6' of 16-gauge craft wire

1" overlap

Duct tape

B. 2"

Duct-tape wrapping

C. Bend wire to create shape.

Fold and use as a template.

5. The next step is to cover the wings with organza fabric. Lay the organza out on a flat surface. Place one of the wings on top of the organza and use a fabric marker to trace around the wing's shape, adding a ¼-in. margin.

6. Using sharp scissors, cut out the wing shape from the fabric. Repeat for the other wing.

7. Before you attach the organza to the wings, you'll need to prep the fabric so that it will conform to the curved shape of the wings when you sew it on in the next step. Set your wire wing on top of the fabric and with your scissors make little snips about every ¼ in. along the perimeter of the fabric, from the edge of the fabric to just where it meets the wire.

continued on p. 52

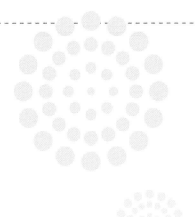

8. Now it's time to get sewing! Thread your needle with about 2 ft. of thread. Begin sewing by folding the fabric over the wire. Holding it in place with one hand, sew the fabric in place, keeping the stitches as close to the wire as possible. You'll be sewing around the wire to help keep it all in place. Repeat for the other wings. You should now have 4 beautiful little wings!

9. Now you get to put the wings together. Lay the top wings on a flat surface. Set the bottom wings on top of them and duct tape them together **(drawing D)**. Cover the duct tape with a wrap of ribbon **(drawing E)**. The end of the ribbon may be sewn into place with a quick stitch or two or a dollop of hot glue.

10. Your pretty princess is going to need a way to wear the wings, so you're going to create straps for the wing frame. To attach the straps, cut 8 in. to 12 in. of ribbon, depending on the size of your

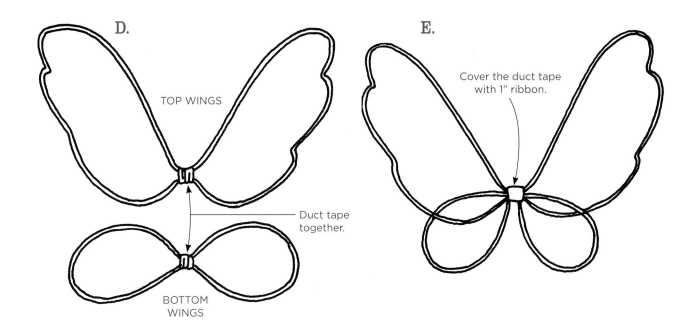

D.

TOP WINGS

Duct tape together.

BOTTOM WINGS

E.

Cover the duct tape with 1" ribbon.

fairy's shoulders, and loop it around the center area of the wings. One strap will go to the left of center, the other to the right. To attach the wings to the wearer, bring the ends of the ribbon loop under her arm and over her shoulder. Tie it in place.

11. To finish up your oh-so-cute wings, place them on a flat surface. Use hot glue to secure the silk flower to the center of the wings for that final embellishment.

DIRECTIONS FOR TUTU

1. The first step, and it's a very important one, is to establish how big you need to make your design. Grab that little fairy princess of yours and take two quick measurements: (a) around the widest part of her belly, and (b) from her waist to the tops of her ankles or to wherever you'd like the bottom of the tutu to fall on her body. I highly recommend not going any lower than the tops of her ankles to help keep tripping to a minimum.

2. Now that you have your measurements, you'll make the waistband of the tutu. Since you're using stretchy elastic for the waistband, you'll need to subtract 2 in. from your flower girl's waist measurement. This ensures the tutu is snug around her waist and stays in place—as much as any garment can stay in place on an active little girl. Cut the desired length from the roll of elastic and sew the ends together with a $\frac{1}{4}$-in. overlap. Hot glue works surprisingly well here if you're sewing-impaired.

3. With scissors or the rotary cutter, cut lengths of tulle that equal double the waist-to-ankle measurement. For example, if the measurement was 20 in., you'll want to cut 40 in. Set the strips aside until you have a large pile ready to go. The more strips you use, the fuller the tutu will be. Adding shorter pieces in the mix will add some fluffiness, too.

continued on p. 54

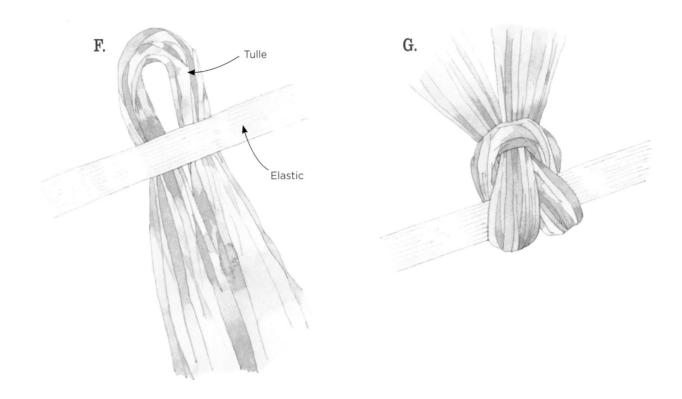

F.

Tulle

Elastic

G.

4. Plop yourself on the sofa in front of your favorite TV show and start assembling the tutu. Slip the elastic band around your thigh. (I know it seems odd, but this helps in getting the right amount of strips on the waistband.) Fold one piece of tulle in half and slip it under the elastic. There will be a loop of tulle at the top of the elastic **(drawing F)**. Now thread the cut ends of the tulle piece through the loop, around the elastic. Pull tight **(drawing G)**. Do this all the way around the elastic band, orienting the knots on the same side of the elastic as you go around, until you have the desired fullness.

tips & hints

- The Internet is a fabulous resource for researching wing shapes. Poke around your favorite search conglomerate's image browser and you'll find hundreds of drawings and pictures to spark your imagination.

- The 16-gauge wire can be found at most hardware stores. Some beading and craft stores will also carry it. Do take note that most wire cutters made for the jewelry hobbyist will be too delicate for the heavier wire. Grab a pair of wire cutters from your hardware store.

- Fabric dyes and paints are great tools for designs, but don't be afraid to try adding glitter glue or flat-back rhinestones or to try using stencils or even spray paint.

- Don't spend a lot of money on panty hose or duct tape. Stop by your local dollar-type discount store and pick them up for $1.00 each.

- Tulle comes in dozens of colors and can be found in the wedding section at most fabric stores. The big box stores will carry basic colors; find the more exotic colors online with a few clicks of your mouse.

- To add something different to your tutu, try incorporating strips of ribbon or beaded trims into the mix.

Price Breakdown

YOUR COST

16-gauge wire	$6.00
Duct tape	$1.00
2 yd. of fabric	$11.00
1 yd. of ribbon	$2.00
Hot glue	$4.00
Silk flower	$3.00
Elastic	$4.00
Tulle ($2.80 x 3)	$8.40

TOTAL	**$39.40**
	for the set

STORE COST

A custom-designed tutu and wings would cost **$60** or more from online vendors.

Bridesmaid Sash

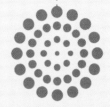

CRAFTY COMMITMENT

2 hours

SOLO A-GO-GO

This solo project is great for a lazy afternoon. Set your iPod℠ on random play and enjoy an afternoon of "me" time.

The first bridesmaid gown I ever wore was for the wedding of one of my distant cousins. It was not so much a gown as it was an embodiment of fashion shame. It was a shade of turquoise so obnoxiously loud that it should only be spelled in ALL CAPS. And, yes, it had a butt bow that made it nearly impossible to sit on a chair. There were nine of us dressed that way, and I'm sure many of us are still dealing with resentment issues to this day.

You, my fashionista darling of a reader, would never do such a thing to your maids. You're the type who has taken every one of your maids' preferences, body issues, and figure types into consideration as you have agonized over the perfect styles to flatter each maid. You've found the perfect dress, but maybe it needs a bit of individuality. Or perhaps you're letting them choose their own gowns and you'd like to add a bit of uniformity. I've got a great little accessory for you that can be personalized to fit your individual maids.

The bridesmaid sash is a beginner-level project that's fun to do. Because ribbon and fabric are available in hundreds of thousands of combinations, this is a perfect project for customizing to suit your color scheme.

SUPPLIES

- 1½-in.-wide double-satin ribbon (you may use thicker or thinner ribbon, depending on the waist measurements of your maids), 1 yd.
- Sharp scissors
- Spray starch
- Iron and ironing board
- Needle and thread to match your ribbon color
- Polyester organza fabrics in the color(s) of your choice, ½ yd. each
- Candle and matches
- Faux pearls of various sizes for centers of flowers
- Sequined and beaded appliqué

A.

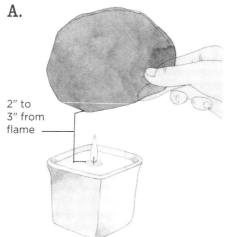

2" to 3" from flame

DIRECTIONS

1. To get started, you'll need the waist measurements of each of your maids. Take that measurement and add 8 in. to establish the length of the ribbon you'll be cutting for the belt. Cut each maid's belt from the spool of ribbon.

2. You'll need to starch and iron the belt to give it some stiffness; otherwise the soft satin ribbon won't hold up well as a belt. Spray the ribbon, per the manufacturer's recommendation, and iron.

3. After the belts have been ironed, the ends need to be hemmed so that there are no rough edges visible. This also helps keep the ribbon from fraying. Fold one end of the ribbon over about ¼ in. Press the iron down on the seam to set it. Repeat on the other side so that you have crisp, even folds. Using your needle and thread, stitch the ends of the ribbon in place with a simple running stitch. Set the belts aside.

4. This is where the creativity begins. It's time to start making flowers. Cut 9 circle shapes from each color of organza. I like using circles from 1 in. to about 5 in. in diameter. I do this freehand because I think it makes more realistic-looking flowers, but you are welcome to trace templates onto the fabric with a fabric pen. I recommend 3 flowers for each belt. You can mix and match colors in each flower or use only 1 color per flower—it's totally up to you.

5. Once you've assembled piles of circles for your flowers, it's time to start the fun part: melting them! Over an open candle flame (a votive candle works fine here), hold the edge of an organza circle 2 in. to 3 in. above the flame until it begins to melt. The fabric will pucker and turn into itself a bit as it melts **(drawing A)**. This is exactly what you want. Be careful here! Once the fabric starts melting, it does so quickly and can burst into flame if you hold it there too long. Rotate the edge of the circle around the flame until the whole flower is melted. Repeat for all layers of the flower.

6. Layer the flower petals on top of each other from largest to smallest, and stitch them together in the center. Add 1 to 3 pearls of various sizes in the center of your flowers by stitching them in with a needle and thread **(drawing B)**.

7. From the sequined and beaded appliqué, clip a swirl or other decorative element with a sharp pair of scissors. This will be positioned behind the flower so that it peeks out a bit, adding that oh-so-fun bit of flair and sparkle to your design.

8. To finish the sash, attach the appliqué piece to the ribbon with a needle and thread. On top of the appliqué and just off-center, attach the flower to the ribbon.

B.

FIT YOUR STYLE

Use gingham ribbon and bright, cheerful colors of organza to create a country-wedding adaptation for your bridesmaids.

tips & hints

- *Organza isn't the only fabric option. Nearly any lightweight polyester fabric can be used. It's important that the fabric is polyester because the synthetic fibers are the ones that melt. Organza, suit linings, some faux taffetas, and silk will work for this project.*

- *Keep a bowl of water nearby in case anything bursts into flames or you burn your fingers. Go ahead; ask me how I know this can happen!*

- *I like doing 8 or 9 layers of circles, but you can do as many—as large or as small—as you like. I caution that anything under 1 in. is generally too small to do anything with, and anything over 6 in. doesn't hold up well.*

Price Breakdown

YOUR COST

1 yd. of ribbon	$5.00
½ yd. of organza (x3)	$12.00
Faux pearls (bag)	$4.00
Appliqué	$6.00
TOTAL	**$27.00**

STORE COST

Handcrafted sashes cost upward of **$50** at specialty bridal vendors.

Bejeweled Bouquet Wrap

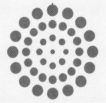

CRAFTY COMMITMENT

15 to 20 minutes

WITH A LITTLE HELP FROM MY FRIENDS

This project can be handed off to a crafty—or even semi-crafty—pal on the wedding day. You're going to be playing the part of princess bride; it's OK to let your loved ones help out.

One of my favorite sayings is, "Do-it-yourself doesn't mean do it all by yourself!" When planning a wedding, it's so easy to get caught up in the excitement of DIY. "Of course I can complete these 30 projects!" you say to yourself. What you may not realize in the early planning stages is that those projects represent hundreds of hours of work on top of your already busy schedule.

I'm an avid advocate of getting a little help when you need it. Sometimes it's gathering a group of buddies for a craft party. Sometimes it's doing partial DIY, taking something premade such as a simple but beautiful bouquet from your florist and embellishing it to create something uniquely you: stunning, romantic, and bejeweled.

This project can be handed off to a crafty—or even semi-crafty—pal on the wedding day and be finished in 15 to 20 minutes. It requires a premade bouquet from your florist. Be sure to order well in advance and request that the florist provide the bouquet with naked stems that are firmly secured with rubber bands or floral wire and ready to wrap.

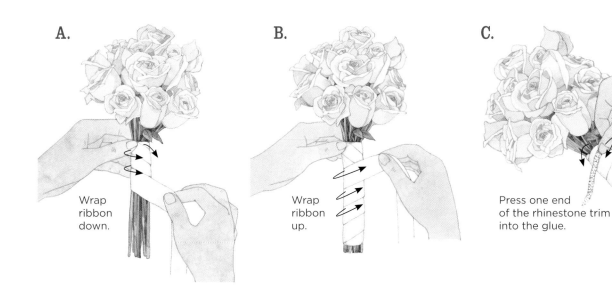

A. Wrap ribbon down.

B. Wrap ribbon up.

C. Press one end of the rhinestone trim into the glue.

SUPPLIES

- Bouquet of your choice, ordered from your florist
- Floral shears
- Scissors
- 1-in-wide white ribbon, 1 yd.
- Floral pins
- Hot glue gun and glue
- 2-row rhinestone trim, 1 yd.
- Wire cutters
- Rhinestone button

DIRECTIONS

1. Ask for your florist to provide your bouquet with naked stems bound with rubber bands or floral wire.

2. If your florist hasn't done so already, cut the stem ends of the bouquet so they are all the same length, 7 in. to 8 in. long. Dry the stems with a paper towel.

3. Cut a length of ribbon about three times as long as the length of the stems, about 24 in. long.

4. Tuck the end of the ribbon inside the top bind, just under the bottoms of the flowers, and start wrapping in a spiral down the length of the stems **(drawing A)**.

5. When you reach the bottom, wrap in a spiral back up the stem **(drawing B)**.

6. At the top, tuck the cut end of the ribbon underneath and secure with a few pins pushed through the ribbon and into the stems.

7. Apply a small dab of hot glue near the bottom of the flowers, on top of the ribbon. Press one end of the rhinestone trim into the glue. Hold it in place until the glue cools and solidifies enough to support the trim **(drawing C)**.

8. Spiral the trim around the bouquet stems until you reach the bottom. Apply another dab of glue and press the rhinestone trim in place. Cut away the excess trim with wire cutters.

9. Just below the first spiral of rhinestones, add the rhinestone button, securing it with a bit of hot glue. You now have a stunning bouquet wrap that looks like a million bucks!

Price Breakdown

YOUR COST

Ribbon	$4.00
Pins	$2.00
Hot glue	$4.00
Rhinestone trim	$14.00
Button	$4.50
TOTAL	**$28.50**

STORE COST

Florists will charge anywhere from **$30** to **$50** for an embellished bouquet wrap.

tips & hints

- *Remember to keep your bouquet in water until you're ready to wrap it.*

- *This is a project that's best done the day of the wedding, preferably no more than an hour before your ceremony. Please hand this off to a trusted helper, with complete instructions, if you've got an already packed morning. (Most of you will.)*

- *Rhinestone trim and buttons can be found at many fabric and notions shops or online.*

- *Rhinestone trim comes in several different configurations and styles, from simple to highly ornate. Of course, the more rhinestones and more complex the design, the more expensive the trim will be.*

- *Online, eBay ® is an excellent source for finding beautiful trims and unique buttons.*

- *Instead of a store-bought button, why not incorporate a piece of heirloom jewelry like an earring or brooch?*

- *A long rhinestone necklace can be used in place of rhinestone trim. Scour secondhand stores for costume jewelry.*

FIT YOUR STYLE

Beach brides can use strands of seashells instead of rhinestones for a fun, quirky alternative. Seashell necklaces can be found online and at party supply stores.

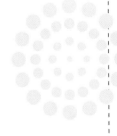

CHAPTER THREE: *Exotic Destinations*

THE RISE OF THE destination wedding over the years has created a tremendous amount of interest in themes that include exotic details and travel-friendly touches. Although many couples may opt to stay closer to home, my goal for this chapter is to present exotic elements that inspire a sense of wanderlust. The idea for using a vintage suitcase and postcards as a guest book was sparked by feeling a bit of nostalgia for the great eras of exploration and tourism. The silk-covered cupcake stand was inspired by rich Indian and Indonesian fabrics. A Havana-inspired cigar box full of tasty treats will give a warm welcome to your out-of-town guests. Tropical locations and their unique florals bring a touch of the exotic with an easy-to-assemble bouquet. For any warm-climate wedding, the palm fans are a must for keeping your guests comfortable. No matter where you decide to get married, you can transport your guests to paradise with a few crafty projects.

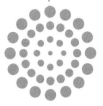

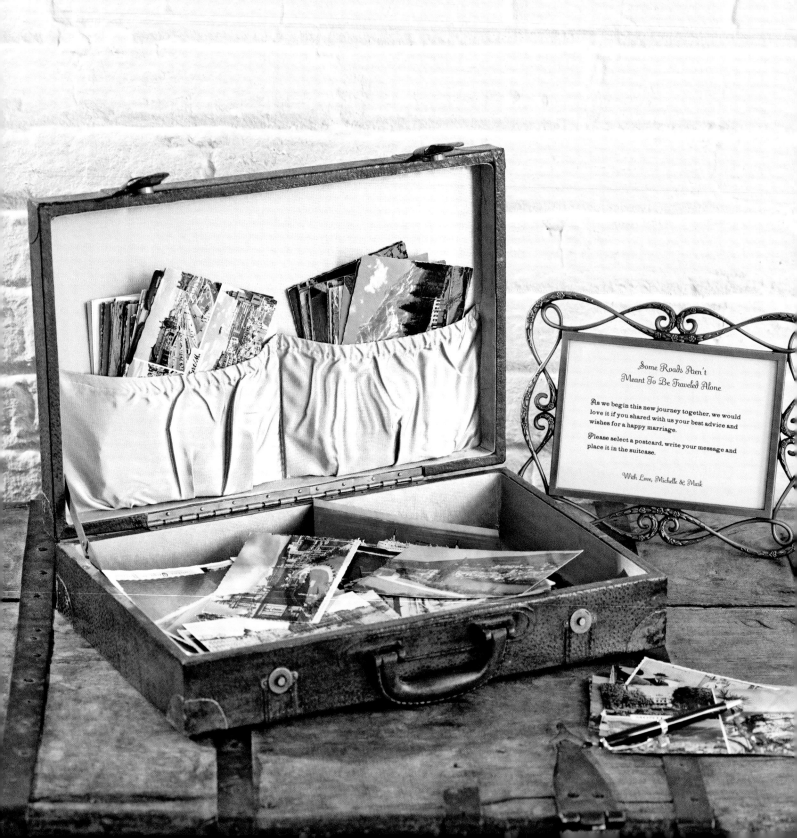

Some Roads Aren't
Meant To Be Traveled Alone

As we begin this new journey together, we would
love it if you shared with us your best advice and
wishes for a happy marriage.

Please select a postcard, write your message and
place it in the suitcase.

With Love, Michelle & Mark

Vintage Luggage Guest Book

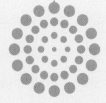

For you travel buffs and lovers of vintage, I've put together this vintage luggage guest "book" idea using a reproduction vintage suitcase, real vintage postcards, a beautiful pen, and a simple sign to direct your guests what to do. It's all very easy to assemble, once you source the materials. I spent a fair amount of time—we're talking weeks here, kids—bidding on unused vintage postcard lots and luggage on eBay. Both are collectibles and can go for big money. Don't get discouraged; sometimes fantastic offers pop up, so you've just got to be patient and have your bid ready at a moment's notice. Allow yourself plenty of time for this project.

If you'd rather recycle used postcards, it can be done! Household bleach and a cotton swab will take most ink off of the back of old postcards. Use a tiny bit of bleach on the swab to "erase" the markings. Another way to use postcards is to scan the front of old cards and print them on precut postcard-size cardstock using your home printer.

CRAFTY COMMITMENT
30 minutes

SOLO A-GO-GO
Putting this project together is a cinch. Set aside a morning, grab some coffee, and enjoy your alone time!

SUPPLIES

- Computer with Microsoft Word
- Printer
- 1 piece of cardstock, cut to 5 in. by 7 in.
- Picture frame, 5 in. by 7 in.
- Vintage postcards
- Vintage or reproduction suitcase
- A lovely pen

FIT YOUR STYLE

Garden-wedding couples could adapt this by using reproductions of vintage seed labels and galvanized pails instead of postcards and luggage.

Price Breakdown

YOUR COST

Cardstock, 1 sheet	$0.30
Picture frame	$12.00
100 postcards	$12.00
Vintage suitcase	$50.00
TOTAL	**$74.30**

STORE COST

I haven't seen any vendors offer this kind of product for sale.

DIRECTIONS

1. The first step is to create a sign that tells your guests what the postcards and suitcase are for. Open up Microsoft Word and create a new document.

2. From the Page Setup menu, select "Custom Page Size" from the "Settings" options. Set the custom page size for "7" wide by "5." Click "OK." Set the margin spacing to "0.25" for the left and right margins. For the top and bottom, set the margin spacing to "0.50." Now, type in your message to your guests. Save. Print onto the cardstock.

3. Open the back of the photo frame and insert your printed direction sheet. This will sit near the signing area.

4. The next step is to go through your postcards and do a quality check. Remove any damaged or unusable ones. If you're making use of used postcards, now is the time to use a bit of bleach on a cotton swab to remove any writing from the back of the cards.

5. The last step is to assemble all of your pieces—suitcase, sign, postcards, and pen—and display them. How easy is that?

tips & hints

- Go beyond suitcases and look for steamer trunks, satchels, or old post office bags for something out of the ordinary.

- Check Grandma's attic for fun luggage.

- The best place to find vintage suitcases and postcards is eBay. It does take some patience to find the right combination of materials in affordable price ranges, so start early and keep your eye out for those one-of-a-kind random deals. They do pop up!

- Check out local pawn shops, secondhand stores, and flea markets for vintage items.

Embellished Raffia Fan

The frantic e-mail came in about a month before the couple's wedding date. "Dear DIY Bride, according to the almanac and local weather archives, our wedding date is going to be a scorcher! How do we keep our guests comfortable during our short-but-still-outdoor ceremony? P.S. We're short on both time and cash."

It's absolutely lovely when brides and grooms are so concerned about the comfort of their guests; that's often overlooked in the hustle and bustle of wedding planning! On hot days when an indoor ceremony isn't possible, I recommend a simple but stylish solution: a hand fan.

Raffia and palm fans can easily be found online for not much money. On their own, they're not much to look at. With just a bit of embellishment like some ribbon and a faux flower, they can be transformed into a wedding-worthy accessory that'll help keep your guests comfy under the afternoon sun.

This is a perfect project for those with no craft experience. Because the fans are a little labor-intensive, grab some pals to make light work of the assembly.

CRAFTY COMMITMENT

10 minutes
per fan

WITH A LITTLE HELP FROM MY FRIENDS

Make quick work of a big project with the helping hands of your friends and family. For maximum efficiency, put someone on cutting duty and the rest on wrapping and embellishing. Treat everyone to light snacks and tropical beverages to get them in the mood.

DIRECTIONS

1. Cut the ribbon into 18-in. lengths. Place a small dollop of hot glue on the front of the fan, just above the loop of the fan handle. Carefully press the end of one of the lengths of ribbon into the hot glue.

2. Wrap the ribbon around the handle of the fan and secure the other end with hot glue when it's covered. It's worth noting that because the fans are handmade, each one may be slightly different. You may not need all 18 in. of ribbon to cover the handle **(drawing A)**.

3. Once the ends are glued down, add another dollop of glue to the front of the fan, over where you began the ribbon wrap, and secure one of the silk orchids. That's all there is to it!

tips & hints

- The silk dupioni is an indulgence. Any other type of ribbon can be used to bring the costs down by half or more.

- Raffia fans are often handmade and created from natural fibers. They're not consistent in size or color, though they are generally pretty close from fan to fan. Don't be surprised if there's some variation in your fans.

- Use any type of silk flower if orchids aren't to your liking.

The best flowers will lie flat, such as a rose in full bloom as opposed to a rosebud.

- Be sure your guests know the fans are available! These look great when one is placed on each guest's chair along with the ceremony program.

- Fans sell out at many vendors during the warm summer months. Be sure to place your order as early as possible to avoid the wedding rush.

SUPPLIES

- ¾-in.-wide silk dupioni ribbon
- Scissors
- Hot glue gun and glue
- 10-in.-wide raffia fans
- Silk orchids, removed from the stems

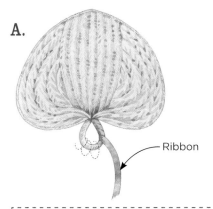

A.

Ribbon

Price Breakdown

YOUR COST

Ribbon (per 40-yd. bolt)	$42.00
Hot glue	$4.00
Raffia fans (80)	$70.00
Silk orchids	$64.00

TOTAL	**$180.00**
	for 80 fans
	or **$2.25** each

STORE COST
Embellished fans can be found at specialty wedding vendors for **$3.00** or more each.

Sari Fabric Cake Stand

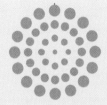

Once considered a fad or novelty at weddings, cupcakes are now so ingrained in our collective dessert culture that they've become a standard option. It's not unusual to see cupcakes at weddings (or any special event).

One of the problems with serving cupcakes in large quantities is how to stylishly display them. There are many different products on the market, from plain cardboard stands to wired candelabra-type holders. Most miss out on style, which I know to be important to you.

I've put together an ambitious project that will hold a hundred or more cupcakes and present them as the treasured jewels they are. For an Indian-inspired affair or for those who want to evoke the exotic, the silk-covered cake stand just may be for you!

A few words of caution about this project: It is labor-intensive and requires that you work with power tools. It's also quite heavy and large; it weighs 40 lb. before the cupcakes are even put on it, and it stands 28 in. tall. I highly recommend having the MDF board cut at your local hardware store so that it's easier to transport home and so that you don't have to invest in expensive tools if they're not already part of your tool box.

CRAFTY COMMITMENT

24 to 48 hours

CRAFTY COUPLE

This is a great project for some couple bonding over your joint DIY prowess! Plan on spending a whole weekend with this one, but do take frequent breaks to chill out. Plan some fun, easy meals to make your time together less stressful.

SUPPLIES

- 2 sheets of ¼-in.-thick MDF, 4 ft. by 8 ft.
- 4-in.-diameter ABS or PVC pipe
- Jigsaw
- ⅜-in.-diameter drill bit and a drill
- Wood glue (Liquid Nails®)
- Hammer
- 1-in. ring-shank nails
- 45-in.-wide silk fabric, 4 yd.
- Spray starch
- Iron
- Spray adhesive
- Sharp knife or screwdriver
- 1 length ⅜-16 "all thread" metal rod
- Four 2-oz. bottles of purple acrylic craft paint

DIRECTIONS

1. To begin, you'll need to cut (or have cut) the MDF to the following dimensions **(drawing A)**:
   - 2 pieces of MDF to 30 in. by 30 in.; these are the top and bottom of layer 1.
   - 2 pieces of MDF to 30 in. by 3½ in.; these are the left and right sides of layer 1.
   - 2 pieces of MDF to 29½ in. by 3½ in.; these are the front and back sides of layer 1.
   - 2 pieces of MDF to 24 in. by 24 in.; these are the top and bottom of layer 2.
   - 2 pieces of MDF to 24 in. by 3½ in.; these are the left and right sides of layer 2.
   - 2 pieces of MDF to 23½ in. by 3½ in.; these are the front and back sides of layer 2.
   - 2 pieces of MDF to 18 in. by 18 in.; these are the top and bottom of layer 3.
   - 2 pieces of MDF to 18 in. by 3½ in.; these are the left and right sides of layer 3.
   - 2 pieces of MDF to 17½ in. by 3½ in.; these are the left and ride sides of layer 3.
   - 2 pieces of MDF to 12 in. by 12 in.; these are the top and bottom of layer 4.
   - 2 pieces of MDF to 12 in. by 3½ in.; these are left and right sides of layer 4.
   - 2 pieces of MDF to 11½ in. by 3½ in.; these are the front and back sides of layer 4.

2. Cut 3 pieces of PVC pipe to 4 in. tall. The top and bottom cuts must be parallel or the tiers will be off balance. This is the trickiest part of the project: You'll need to make inserts, or disks, for each end of the pieces of pipe out of pieces of MDF board left over from the box layers. The easiest way to do this is to take a pencil and trace the inside circumference of the pipe directly on a piece

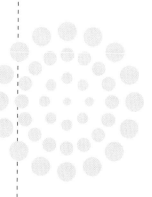

A.

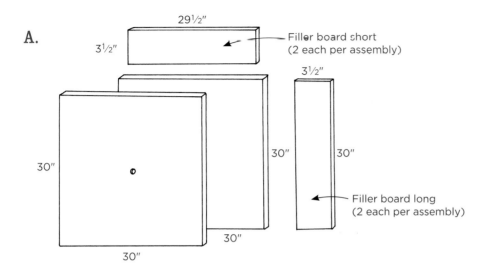

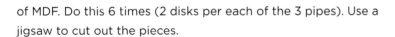

29½"

3½"

Filler board short
(2 each per assembly)

3½"

30"

30"

30"

30"

Filler board long
(2 each per assembly)

30"

30"

of MDF. Do this 6 times (2 disks per each of the 3 pipes). Use a jigsaw to cut out the pieces.

3. Next, holes will need to be drilled in the center of each MDF disk using the ⅜-in. drill bit. All of the holes must be in the same location on each disk. The pipes act as supports for each layer of the cake stand. The center holes are a guide to keep a metal rod in place so that everything remains level and secure. Once you drill a hole in the first disk, you can use this as a template for drilling the other pieces.

4. Now set the disks into the pipe ends. Using Liquid Nails, add a ring around the outer edge of three of the disks. Take these disks and place them on a level surface. Slide the end of a pipe over each one. The seal should be snug. Allow the Liquid Nails to dry, 24 hours or according to the manufacturer's recommendation. Once dry, flip the pipes over and repeat with the remaining three disks.

5. After the pipes have set up, you may go ahead and paint them to coordinate with your fabric. Set aside and allow them to dry.

continued on p. 76

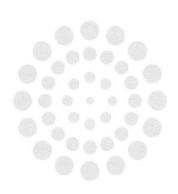

B.

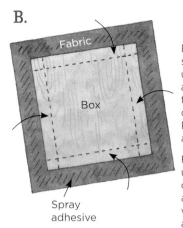

Fabric

Box

Bring one side of fabric up the side and over the bottom of the box. Repeat for all sides.

Fold over unattached corners and adhere with spray adhesive

Spray adhesive

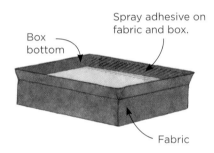

Spray adhesive on fabric and box.

Box bottom

Fabric

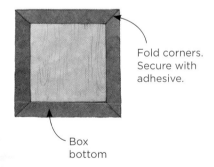

Fold corners. Secure with adhesive.

Box bottom

6. The next part is fairly involved but not terribly difficult. We'll be assembling the layers of the cake stand now. Start off by drilling holes with the $\frac{3}{8}$-in. drill bit in the center of the top and bottom of each layer. (A quick way to find the exact center? Use a straightedge and a pencil to draw a line from corner to corner on all 4 corners. Where the lines connect is the center. Boom! Easy.)

7. Set the top of layer 1 on a flat surface. Using a generous amount of Liquid Nails, glue the right and left side pieces to the top of the board. Hammer the shank nails, one near each corner, into each of the sides from the top to secure the pieces into place. Let the glue dry. Add the front and back pieces; allow to dry. Then add the bottom piece on top of the sides. Again, allow the glue to dry. Repeat for all layers. The hardest parts are now done. You are a cupcake tower construction deity. Behold your awesomeness!

8. Now, let's get those naked tiers covered with that beautiful fabric. Lay out the fabric on a smooth surface. Measure out the following dimensions and cut:
   - 35 in. by 35 in. for layer 1
   - 29 in. by 29 in. for layer 2
   - 23 in. by 23 in. for layer 3
   - 17 in. by 17 in. for layer 4

   (It's the layer width + 5 in. by height + 5 in. in case you're using alternative layer sizes at home.)

9. Spray each piece of fabric with spray starch and iron it to crispy perfection. The smoother and more wrinkle-free your fabric, the easier it'll be for you to decorate your boxes.

10. Set one box on a flat surface and spray a light, even layer of spray adhesive. Center one piece of fabric on top, making sure there's even overlay on all sides, and smooth it down across the board.

11. Flip the box over, fabric side down, and spray a layer of adhesive directly on the fabric flaps that are facing upward (toward you). Bring one side up the side and over the bottom of the box; it will extend only 1½ in. inward. The undersides of the boxes are not totally covered. Repeat for all sides of the box. You'll notice you have unattached corner pieces. That's exactly what you should be seeing. To deal with these, fold them to either side (left or right). They should lay flat, without any overhang. Spray the underside of one side with adhesive and press it firmly in place to secure it. Repeat for all sides. Now, repeat this process for the remaining 3 layers **(drawing B)**.

12. Remember the holes you drilled? Those have been covered by fabric. You'll need a sharp knife or even a screwdriver to poke a hole through the fabric to make way for the metal rod.

13. Final assembly! Place layer 1 on your display table. Slip in the metal rod. Now, slide on one of the PVC spacers. Add layer 2, another spacer, layer 3, another spacer, and then layer 4. You did it! You created a couture-worthy custom cake stand **(drawing C)**. How proud are you right now?

tips & hints

- You can use nearly any opaque fabric to suit your style and budget. Polyester taffeta, crisp linen, synthetic satin, and poly-blend velvet are all luxe-on-a-budget alternatives.

- Not sold on using fabric? Try a daring wallpaper or even a beautiful paint (be sure to prime the wood before adding a latex-based paint).

- The boxes can be made to any size, and you can use as many or as few tiers as you need; it's totally up to you!

- Your local home improvement store or lumberyard will often cut the boards for you for a nominal fee. Account for this in your budget and be sure they're cutting to your exact measurements.

Price Breakdown

YOUR COST

MDF board	$20.00
PVC pipe	$15.00
Liquid Nails	$10.00
Hardware	$5.00
Fabric	$40.00
Spray starch	$4.00
Adhesive	$8.00
Rod	$13.00
Paint	$4.00
TOTAL	**$119.00**

STORE COST
Paper-covered cardboard cake stands cost around **$120.00** from designers.

C.

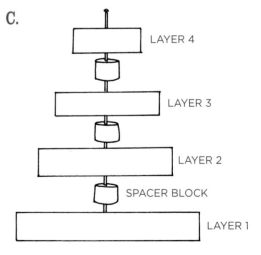

LAYER 4
LAYER 3
LAYER 2
SPACER BLOCK
LAYER 1

A. Layer 1	E. Add spacer
B. Screw in rod	F. Add layer 3
C. Add spacer	G. Add Spacer
D. Add layer 2	H. Add Layer 4

Mojito
Cookies

Plantain
Chips

Cuban
Snack

Rothschilds

IMPORTED

HAND MADE

welcome to
our wedding

Cigar Box Welcome Package

For years, Cuba has held a near-mythical allure for me. I love the cuisine, I love the music, and, at one time, I loved the cigars. (Yes, I'm a reformed cigar aficionado!) Instead of collecting cigars, I'm now a purveyor of beautiful cigar boxes. They're so perfect for crafting and, oh, the intoxicating scent of a fine cigar is utterly divine.

For my fellow Cubaphiles, this cigar box project makes a lovely welcome package for your out-of-town guests. Each cigar box holds little Cuban-inspired snacks, a local map, and a handwritten note on a cigar label–inspired card. To help you save time and cash, the snacks are a combination of premade and handmade. You'll get to show off some culinary skill while taking a few sanity-saving shortcuts. You'll be making mojito cookies and a Cuban-spice snack mix. Your shortcut snack is store-bought plantain chips.

Cigar boxes come in many different shapes and sizes and can be purchased directly from cigar shops for a few dollars each. Online sites eBay and Etsy[SM] are also excellent places to find them in bulk for not a lot of money. The downside of shopping online is that you'll have to pay shipping costs.

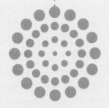

CRAFTY COMMITMENT
10 hours

CRAFTY COUPLE
If your beloved is a foodie, this is a fun way to spend some quality time together in the kitchen. Schedule a day to put your culinary skills to use and enjoy each other's company. Have fun!

Welcome Package Recipes

SUPPLIES

For Mojito Cookies
Makes approx. 2 dozen cookies

1/2	cup butter
3/4	cup sugar, plus more for topping
1	whole egg
1 1/2	Tbs. rum extract
1	lime, zested
1 1/2	Tbs. lime juice
1	tsp. mint extract
1 3/4	cups all-purpose flour
1	tsp. baking soda

For Cuban-Spice Snack Mix
Makes approx. 18 servings

1	tsp. cumin
1	tsp. oregano
1	tsp. garlic powder
1	tsp. grated orange zest
1	tsp. grated lemon zest
1/2	cup butter or margarine
2	Tbs. Worcestershire sauce
3	cups Wheat Chex® cereal
2	cups Rice Chex® square cereal
1 1/2	cups peanuts
1 1/2	cups small pretzel rods

DIRECTIONS FOR MOJITO COOKIES

1. In a large bowl, combine the butter and sugar, mixing it until it is a creamy consistency. Add the egg and beat until the mixture is fluffy. Add the rum extract, lime zest, lime juice, and mint extract. Mix until well combined.

2. In a separate bowl, sift together the flour and baking soda. Add them to the wet ingredients and combine until just mixed.

3. Divide the dough into 2 equal parts. Place each piece onto a sheet of plastic wrap and roll into a log. Refrigerate the log overnight or freeze for 1 hour to chill and harden.

4. Preheat the oven to 350° F. Line baking sheets with parchment paper. Remove the cookie dough from the refrigerator and peel away the plastic wrap. Slice the rolls into 1/4-in.-thick rounds and place them on the parchment-lined sheets, 3 across and 4 down. Sprinkle the tops with sugar and bake for 14 to 16 minutes, until the cookies are golden brown.

5. Remove the cookies from the pan and place them on a cooling rack for about 10 minutes. Let them cool completely before packaging them.

DIRECTIONS FOR CUBAN-SPICE SNACK MIX

1. Preheat the oven to 275° F. Mix the cumin, oregano, garlic powder, orange zest, and lemon zest together in a small bowl.

2. Melt the butter in a shallow saucepan. Stir the Worcestershire sauce and the spice mix into the butter.

3. In a large bowl, mix the Chex cereals, peanuts, and pretzel rods. Stir in the butter-spice mix until all the pieces are coated.

4. Place the cereal mix in a shallow baking pan. Bake for 40 minutes, stirring every 10 minutes. Allow to cool completely before packaging.

DIRECTIONS TO ASSEMBLE THE PACKAGE

1. Fill bags with cookies, snack mix, and plantain chips.

2. With the paper punch, punch out 3 labels from a sheet of sticker paper. On each label, write the contents of each of the bags. Fold the tops of the bags down and attach the corresponding label to keep them sealed.

3. Download the cigar label template from www.diybride.com. Print it on a 5-in. by 7-in. piece of white cardstock. Write a cheerful welcome to your guests. Place the card, the treats, and the map in the box. Tie it with a pretty ribbon and it's ready for giving!

tips & hints

- *To help ensure all of your goodies are fresh on the day of delivery, it's best to make all of your treats no more than 2 to 3 days before giving them to your guests.*

- *The snacks created for this project are merely a (tasty) suggestion. You can put what-ever yummy treats you desire into the box. If you're known for a specific snack recipe, this is a perfect opportunity to flex your culinary muscle.*

- *Finding bulk cigar boxes that are all of the same size can be a challenge. Most bulk lots have a variety of sizes. Your best bet, if you're going for consistency, is to stalk your local cigar shops. Let the owner know you're in the market for a specific size. Many will be happy to set them aside for you as they become available. Allow yourself plenty of time to collect enough for your list of recipients.*

- *I realize that not everyone is as fond of the scent of cigars as I am. Unfortunately, there aren't any good ways of removing the cigar smell com-pletely from a box. Sometimes sprinkling them with baking soda and leaving them to sit for a few days will help remove some of the smell. Remember to empty the baking soda before giving the boxes away!*

SUPPLIES

- Cellophane bags, 4 in. by 6 in.
- Mojito Cookies
- Cuban-Spice Snack Mix
- Plantain chips
- Scalloped rectangle paper punch, 1 in. by 2 in.
- Sticker paper
- Label card template; download at www.diybride.com
- Computer and printer
- White cardstock, cut to 5 in. by 7 in.
- Local map
- Cigar box, about 3 in. deep
- Ribbon

Price Breakdown

YOUR COST

Cookies, per dozen bags	$3.75
Snack mix, per dozen bags	$2.00
Plantain chips, per dozen bags	$2.50
Sticker paper	$4.00
Cardstock, per dozen notes	$2.00
Maps	$3.00
Cigar boxes, per dozen	$36.00
Ribbon	$4.00

TOTAL	**$57.25**
	per dozen or
	$4.77 each

STORE COST

Specialty vendors offer pre-assembled out-of-town baskets for **$20** and up.

Tropical Flower Bouquet

If you're dreaming of a wedding held on the beaches of Hawaii but your budget necessitates that you stay close to home in Wisconsin, don't fret. While I can't help you transform Madison into Maui, I can show you how to invoke the feeling of an exotic tropical location—even if you're ankle-deep in snow.

Using flowers and plants is one of the easiest and most effective ways to add the feeling of a lush, exotic climate to your wedding decor. This beautiful and utterly tropical bouquet uses bright, fiery colors and bold organic shapes to conjure the sense of being on a warm, off-the-beaten-path hideaway.

Though tropical flowers may seem like they'd be more difficult to find than popular local flowers, that's not the case. The oh-so-glorious Internet makes it possible for couples anywhere from Portland, Oregon, to Portland, Maine, to have year-round access to gorgeous, affordable flora from far-off locations with just a few clicks of the mouse.

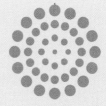

CRAFTY COMMITMENT

2 hours

WITH A LITTLE HELP FROM MY FRIENDS

On the big day, hand off the floral arranging to a trusted friend or two while you're off being a beautiful bride.

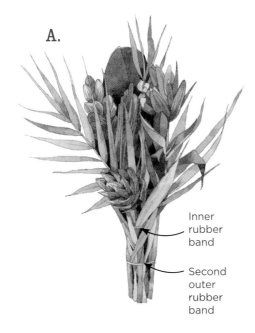

A.

Inner rubber band

Second outer rubber band

SUPPLIES

- 3 stems orange birds of paradise
- 1 stem Jacqunii Heliconia
- 1 to 3 stems purple dendrobium blooms
- Rubber bands
- 4 stems pink ginger
- 2 to 4 standard Areca palm leaves
- 2 to 4 palm fronds
- 4 to 6 red ti leaves
- 1 Anthurium leaf
- Floral shears
- Floral pins
- Bucket of water

DIRECTIONS

1. This project looks more complex than it really is. Essentially what you're doing is putting together a small group of flowers and foliage, securing them with a rubber band, adding the remaining flora, using rubber bands to hold it all in place, and finishing it off with a ti leaf wrap. So let's get started! Gather together 1 stalk each of the bird of paradise, Jacqunii Heliconia, and dendrobium blooms. Secure them with a rubber band, just tight enough to hold them together without damaging the stems. This is your bouquet center.

2. Working your way around the center, add one each of the remaining stems of flowers and foliage, alternating the colors and types as you go along. When you've made one full revolution of the center, add another rubber band to hold it all in place. **(drawing A)**. Add a third layer of flowers and foliage; secure it with a rubber band.

3. Now is the time to do some rearranging and fuss with the design a bit if you'd like. You may feel some of the palms need to be trimmed or that you need to raise the florals a bit so they can be seen better; that's OK! This is the same process florists go through. If needed, add more flowers, remove some foliage, or do whatever will help the bouquet look balanced and proportional.

4. Once you're satisfied with the design, it's time to trim the stems. A stem length of 8 in. to 12 in. is sufficient for most brides. This gives adequate real estate to hold on to without too much overhang beyond your hands.

5. Use another rubber band about ¼ in. from the bottom of the cut stems to hold them in place.

6. Slip the end of a ti leaf into the bottom rubber band and wrap the remaining part of the leaf upward around the stems **(drawing B)**. Secure the end with a floral pin. If you need to, add another leaf or two to finish covering the stems, securing them in place with floral pins.

7. Keep the bouquet in a warm place in about 3 in. of water until ceremony time.

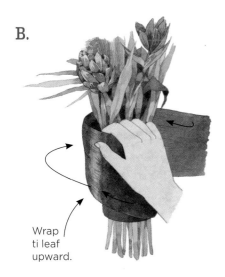

B.

Wrap ti leaf upward.

tips & hints

- *Tropicals are available year-round from florists and Internet floral retailers.*

- *While the florals and foliage are generally inexpensive, shipping from tropical climates can add up quickly. Do factor shipping costs into your budget, and shop around for the best rates.*

- *Most tropicals will need to be kept in room temperature water and in a warm room. This isn't a project for cold basements or chilly garages.*

- *This is a project that's best done the day before or the day of the wedding. Please hand this off to a trusted helper, with complete instructions, if you've got an already packed morning. (Most of you will.)*

- *The ti leaf wrap can be substituted with a beautiful silk or satin ribbon.*

- *If palm leaves aren't to your liking, ferns or grasses may be substituted for a more delicate-looking arrangement.*

Price Breakdown

YOUR COST

Birds of paradise	$4.00
Jacqunii Heliconia	$7.00
Dendrobium	$6.00
Ginger	$7.00
Palm leaves and fronds	$6.00
Ti leaves	$6.00
Anthurium	$6.00
Floral pins	$3.00
TOTAL	**$45.00**

STORE COST

Custom bouquets cost upward of **$80.00** each.

CHAPTER FOUR: *Winter Wonderland*

IF YOU GO weak in the knees for cold-weather weddings, this chapter is sure to hold a warm place in your heart. Whether you're whisking everyone away to a mountain lodge for a wedding and ski weekend or are staying close to home during the winter months, I wanted to create fun, cozy projects that evoked the sense of a winter wonderland no matter where you got married. The quilled snowflake save-the-dates and pinecone-studded bouquet would be delightful for snowy weddings in the mountains. The baby's breath centerpieces add a snow flurry effect to your table. Adorn your maids with a gorgeous pearl and crystal necklace that adds the perfect amount of sparkle to a winter fete. Don't forget to send your guests away with yummy peppermint hot chocolate favors to end a perfect day.

Peppermint Cocoa

Mix contents in large bowl
with 2 2/3 cups of boiling water.

Serves 2.

With love,

Jeff and Bill

Hot Chocolate Favor

Some of my favorite holiday presents to make are edible gift kits packaged in jars. And let me assure you that this hot chocolate kit is a clear winner amongst my recipients. Who can resist a nice cup of hot cocoa on a chilly winter's day? Think about it: luscious, rich chocolate melted into a delicious cream and sweet marshmallow base with just a touch of peppermint to perk it up. Mmmmm! Are your taste buds tingling yet?

Cold weather weddings are the perfect occasion to give a hot chocolate kit as a favor. Your guests will love the yummy treat when they get home (just add water!), and you'll love how cost-effective and simple these are to put together. Better yet, even those of us with few culinary skills can create these very special treats!

This recipe can be scaled to fit any size jar or container and is easily modified to include your favorite chocolate combinations. If peppermint isn't your favorite, how about adding chocolate-covered espresso beans? Replace the powdered milk with powdered flavored nondairy creamer for something extra-fun. Add a tag, tie some ribbon around the jar, and you have a tasty, crowd-pleasing favor. How easy is that?

CRAFTY COMMITMENT

10 minutes
per favor

CRAFTY COUPLE

Even the least crafty groom-to-be can get on board with this project. Grab your guy and set him to the task of measuring and pouring while you add the finishing touches. Or vice versa!

SUPPLIES

(Makes 1 favor)

- 1 clear glass jar, pint size
- ½ cup sugar
- ½ cup unsweetened cocoa powder
- ½ cup powdered milk
- Pinch of salt
- Mini marshmallows
- Crushed peppermint candies
- Mini chocolate chips
- Tape measure
- 2-in.-wide ribbon in brown
- Scissors
- Double-sided tape
- 1-in.-wide ribbon in mint
- Computer with Microsoft Word
- Printer
- Cardstock, 8½ in. by 11 in.
- Hole punch
- Twine

A.

FIT YOUR STYLE

Hot chocolate out of season for your wedding? No problem! Jars can be used to package homemade lemonade mix, cookie mixes, spice mixes, or granola.

DIRECTIONS

1. The instructions for filling the jar are ridiculously easy: Layer sugar, cocoa powder, powdered milk, and salt in the jar **(drawing A)**.

2. Add a layer of mini marshmallows, a layer of crushed peppermint candies, and top with a layer of chocolate chips to finish the yummy goodness. Seal the jars.

3. Measure around the circumference of the jar. Cut a piece of brown 2-in. ribbon to length.

4. To secure the ribbon, place a small piece of double-sided tape on the jar. Wrap the ribbon around the jar, pressing the ends onto the double-sided tape.

5. Cut a length of mint-colored ribbon twice as long as the brown ribbon. Wrap the ribbon around the jar, centering over the brown ribbon, and tie it into a pretty bow.

6. Now it's time to create a tag so that your guests know how to prepare the hot chocolate mix when they get home. Open Microsoft Word and create a new "8.5" by "11" document.

7. From the drawing toolbar, select the text box icon. Click on the document and drag your mouse to create a text box that's 2 in. wide by 3 in. long. Click inside the text box and create a personal message for your guests. The instructions for cocoa preparation are "Mix contents in a large bowl with $2\frac{2}{3}$ cups boiling water. Makes 2 servings."

8. Save and print your document on the cardstock. Cut out the tags with scissors, punch a small hole in the top, and tie the tag to the metal closure of the jar using the twine.

Price Breakdown

YOUR COST

Jars for 12 favors	$36.00
Cocoa	$3.50
Powdered milk	$1.00
Mini marshmallows	$2.00
Peppermint candies	$1.00
Chocolate chips	$1.50
Ribbon	$3.00
Tape	$2.00
Cardstock	$1.00
TOTAL	**$51.00**

for 12 favors or **$4.25** each

STORE COST

Basic favors of hot chocolate packets cost **$3.00** or more from online boutiques.

tips & hints

- The saying "quality in, quality out" applies here. The better your ingredients, the better the hot chocolate will be. National brand ingredients will be perfectly fine—and delicious—for most. If you want to go a bit upscale, opt for hand-made marshmallows, Dutch-processed cocoa, and artisan chocolates.

- These can be made a few weeks in advance. Keep the jars sealed and store them in a cool, dry place until you're ready to give them away.

- Ribbon is a simple and cost-effective embellishment for your jar. It comes in hundreds of colors and widths so that you can mix and match to your wedding's color theme.

- Nondairy powdered creamers can be used in place of the powdered milk. Nondairy creamers come in a multitude of different flavors that'd be yummy when combined with chocolate.

- The best prices for glass jars are generally found at online specialty retailers who offer bulk discounts to customers. Beware that glass is heavy and expensive to ship, so always inquire about shipping costs before you order. That great deal may not be so great when you factor in the transportation costs.

- Don't limit yourself to just hot chocolate for your favors! You can scale your favorite cookie recipes, create spiced tea mixes, or add ready-to-eat granola as an alternative any time of the year. Remember to use dry ingredients only and include directions and a list of further ingredients for your guests.

Quilled Snowflake Save-the-Date

As a crafter, I get so excited when old, nearly forgotten crafting techniques make their way into the mainstream. In the paper-crafting community, quilling is one of those crafts that are beginning to make their way back into favor.

Quilling is simply putting together rolled pieces of paper or cardstock to create intricate shapes. I've seen everything from detailed florals to gorgeous text created by quilling artists. Quilling lends itself to the creation of delicate and ornate designs that epitomize the wintery feel of dainty, one-of-a-kind snowflakes.

Though quilling isn't a difficult craft to master, it does take a lot of patience! Give yourself plenty of time to complete each step in this project; it's not one I'd leave until the last minute because of the detail that goes into each part.

Have fun with this one and take pride in knowing that you're keeping alive a craft tradition that nearly died out. Now, if we can only find a way to bring back macramé!

CRAFTY COMMITMENT

5 hours
per 25 cards

WITH A LITTLE HELP FROM MY FRIENDS

Make quick work of a big project with the helping hands of your friends and family. Put someone on cutting duty and the rest to work on quilling, assembly, and embellishment. Treat everyone to yummy hot toddies when it's all done.

SUPPLIES

- White cardstock, pearl white, 10 in. by 5 in.
- Double-sided tape
- Silver cardstock, $4^3/4$ in. by $4^3/4$ in.
- Blue cardstock, $4^1/2$ in. by $4^1/2$ in.
- Lightweight white cardstock (under 80 lb.), 12 in. by 12 in., found at craft and scrapbook stores
- Paper cutter
- Quilling tool, found at craft stores
- Liquid paper adhesive
- Spray adhesive
- Glitter

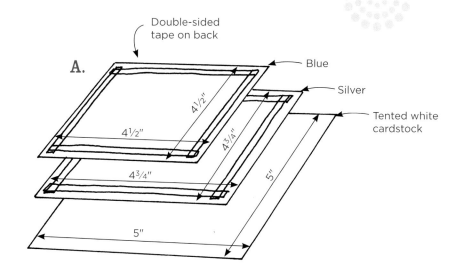

A. Double-sided tape on back · Blue · Silver · Tented white cardstock · $4^1/2"$ · $4^1/2"$ · $4^3/4"$ · $4^3/4"$ · $5"$ · $5"$

DIRECTIONS

1. The easiest way to get started is to set up your card bases. Fold the 10-in. by 5-in. white cardstock in half to create a 5-in. by 5-in. tented card. Apply double-sided tape to the back of the silver cardstock and adhere it to the front of the white card, centering it top to bottom and left to right. Now, add double-sided tape to the back of the blue cardstock and, centering it, adhere that to the front of the silver cardstock. You now have a very pretty base to attach the gorgeous snowflake that you'll be making next **(drawing A)**.

2. This is the fun part! Cut a piece of the lightweight 12-in. by 12-in. white cardstock into ¼-in.-wide strips. From these strips, you'll need to cut the following lengths:
   - 5 strips of 6 in. long
   - 12 strips of 3 in. long
   - 4 strips of 2 in. long

3. Take a strip of 6-in. by ¼-in. cardstock and insert the end into the opening at the end of the quilling tool. Bring the tool to the end of the paper and beginning rolling the paper around the end of the tool. Roll it all the way up and then let go. The circle will loosen a bit; that's OK. Apply a tiny bit of liquid paper adhesive to the loose end and glue it down on the body of the circle. Remove the piece from the quilling tool. This piece will serve as the center of your snowflake. The remaining quills will build upon it **(photo A)**.

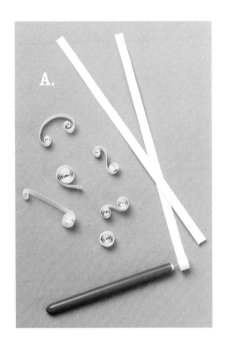

4. The next step is to create small teardrop shapes. This is done by creating circles (as you've just done in the previous step) and pinching one end. Roll one of the 3-in. strips on the quilling tool. Adhere the loose end to the body and remove the piece from the quilling tool. Using your index finger and thumb, pinch one end of the circle to create a teardrop shape. Create 4 teardrop shapes for this snowflake. **(drawing B)**

5. You'll now make a marquis shape. It's a circle with both ends flattened to create a shape that looks like an eye. Roll one of the 2 in. strips onto the quilling tool. Adhere the loose end to the body and remove the piece from the quilling tool. Using your thumb and index finger, pinch one side to create a teardrop, then pinch the other side. Create 4 marquis shapes for this snowflake.

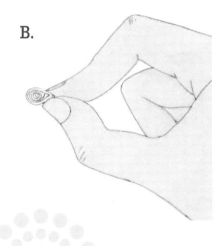

6. The next step is to create scrolls. Gently fold a 6-in. strip in half. Roll each end toward the fold. It'll end up looking like a fancy heart. You'll need 4 scrolls.

7. Now we're going to create the arms. The arms are made from the 3-in. strips. Roll 1 end around the quilling tool, about 3 full turns. Release it from the quilling tool and roll the other end about 12 times, until the total length of the piece is about 1 in. long. Release it from the tool. Repeat on another 3-in. strip.

continued on p. 96

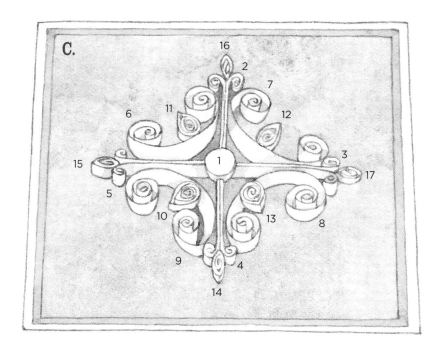

You're almost done! To finish up the arms, you'll need to glue
2 pieces back-to-back to create a single arm. You'll need a total
of 4 arms.

8. The quilling part is done! It's time to assemble all of your pretty
    rolled paper into a beautiful snowflake. Let's start with the center
    piece, the first round you created **(1 on drawing C)**. Using liquid
    paper adhesive, glue the arm pieces at the widest end, to the
    center circle **(2–5 on drawing C)**. The edges of the loops should
    be butted next to each other.

9. Next, take a scroll and glue it onto those small loops of the arms
    (6–9 on drawing C). Gently pull the scroll out until it touches the
    arms. Glue the pieces together where they meet.

10. Take one of the teardrops and glue it to the middle of the scroll
    (10–13 on drawing C). Gently pull the scrolls over to meet the

teardrop, and glue them together. It's OK to unravel the scrolls and bend them a bit at this point to get them to meet the other pieces of quilling. Repeat on all sides.

11. The final touch is to glue the marquis pieces into the indentations at the top of the loops of each arm **(14–17 on drawing C)**.

12. In a well-ventilated place, spray the snowflakes with spray aerosol adhesive and sprinkle with glitter. Shake off the excess glitter. Voilà! You have a beautiful, intricate snowflake to attach to the front of your card with a bit of double-sided tape.

tips & hints

- *Cardstocks and papers come in thousands of colors and patterns. The best spots for finding beautiful and even trendy designs are at scrapbook and art stores.*

- *It's best to use lightweight cardstocks and papers for quilling. If the cardstock is too heavy, it will bend and fold rather than creating a pretty spiral.*

- *Glitters come in all sorts of colors and textures. The best textures for the snowflakes are lightweight, fine-to-medium ground glitters. Chunky glitters are typically too heavy for such an intricate project.*

- *Not into glitter? That's A-OK! The snowflakes look gorgeous without it.*

- *Quilling tools can be found at better-stocked craft stores and online. If you want to save a few bucks and make your own, I've seen crafters split the pointy ends of bamboo skewers to create their own tool.*

Price Breakdown

YOUR COST

Cardstock	**$20.00**
Quilling tool	**$5.00**
Adhesives/tape	**$15.00**
Glitter	**$8.00**

TOTAL	**$48.00**
	for 25 or **$1.92** each

STORE COST

Custom quilled snowflake ornaments alone cost anywhere from **$4.00** to **$5.00** each at craft boutiques.

Baby's Breath Centerpiece

Mention baby's breath to most brides and immediately their thoughts go to cheapy Valentine's bouquets and circa-1980s weddings. But not anymore!

Baby's breath has been seeing a resurgence in the weddingsphere, not as an afterthought or filler flower but rather as the main attraction. Delicate and lacy, it's a flower that, when used in large arrangements, makes a statement. It becomes classic, not frumpy or dated.

This project is one of the simplest in the entire book. It's friendly to the uncraftiest of would-be crafters. Assembly is a cinch and it's easy on the budget. Baby's breath, with its light, snowy feel, is the perfect addition to a wintery table. What's not to love?

Because baby's breath is so fragile, it's best to buy locally, if you can, so that it doesn't have to endure shipping. (It's usually much cheaper to buy it that way, too.) If you can't find it locally, there are a number of online floral outlets that sell baby's breath for reasonable prices.

For a make-a-statement centerpiece, I recommend using two big bunches of baby's breath per vase. If the bunches are on the small side, use three or more. The bigger, the better!

CRAFTY COMMITMENT

30 minutes per floral arrangement

WITH A LITTLE HELP FROM MY FRIENDS

On the big day, hand off the floral arranging to a few trusted helpers while you're off being a blissful, beautiful bride.

SUPPLIES

- 3 tall white vases, 14 in. or more in height
- Water
- Large bunches of fresh baby's breath, 2 per container
- Floral tape
- Floral shears

DIRECTIONS

1. Fill your vases three-quarters full with cool tap water.

2. Combine 2 bunches of baby's breath together with floral tape about halfway down the stalks.

3. Trim the stalks to make them even and to provide a fresh cut to help them absorb water and stay fresh.

4. Place the bundle of flowers into the vases. You may need to do some minor trimming of the bundles to form them into a unified shape at this point.

5. Place the vases on the table. Seriously, friends, that's it! Aren't you proud of yourself?

FIT YOUR STYLE

Baby's breath can be easily adapted to other themes. Try it with rope-wrapped bud vases for beach weddings or skinny, faux mercury glass vases for modern affairs.

tips & hints

- Baby's breath should be purchased 2 to 3 days before your event. Keep it in a cool, dry place in a large bucket (a 5-gallon one found at your local hardware store is excellent) with about 3 in. of water in the bottom.

- There are different varieties of baby's breath on the market. I like New Love for its fullness and quantity of flowers. It's fuller than what you'd typically buy at the supermarket or receive in a generic arrangement.

- Head's up! Since flowers are a product of Mother Nature, they will have some variation from bunch to bunch and flower to flower. That's normal and part of their charm.

- Your local florist, flower market, or grocery store floral department can often special-order baby's breath in bulk for you. Just ask!

- Baby's breath, also known as Gypsophila, is available year-round.

Price Breakdown

YOUR COST

Vases (3)	**$30.00**
Baby's breath (6 bunches)	**$24.00**
Floral tape	**$3.00**

TOTAL $57.00
per 3-vase centerpiece

STORE COST
Florists will charge **$60** to **$120** for a similar centerpiece.

Pinecone Bouquet

Floral design seems like a big, scary project, but it doesn't have to be. The key to bouquet success is to select hardy flowers that are available year-round, have the proper tools on hand, have a helper to assemble, and choose a simple design that doesn't take a lot of fussing.

For a winter bouquet, I wanted to bring you something that was soft, feminine, and wintery but that didn't have any kind of holiday vibe to it. So I used a touch of pink and purple combined against a white backdrop with a surprise addition of pinecones. It's a lovely balance of colors and textures without being too complicated.

OK, would-be florists, here's the deal with DIY flowers: They must be done as close to ceremony time as possible in order for them to stay fresh throughout your wedding day. This takes some planning and, ideally, someone else to do the work for you on the day of the wedding because you're already going to be incredibly busy.

This project takes a full hour to put together if you create the pinecone picks ahead of time. It's best to order your flowers to arrive 2 to 3 days before your wedding. Make sure you have a cool place to store them and containers that can hold enough water for them to stay hydrated while they wait for assembly.

**CRAFTY
COMMITMENT**
1 hour

**WITH
A LITTLE HELP
FROM
MY FRIENDS**
This project
can be handed off to a
crafty—or even semi-crafty
pal—on the wedding day.
Be sure to have all of the
supplies, including the
wired pinecones, ready for
an easy assembly.

SUPPLIES

- 5-gallon bucket and water
- 3 or 4 stems of white hydrangea
- 6 pale pink roses, thorns and leaves removed
- 1 dozen sprigs of pink veronica, available from florists
- Floral shears
- Hot glue gun and glue
- Green floral wire, available at craft stores
- Wire cutters
- 1 dozen small pinecones, 1 in. to 2 in. tall
- Large rubber bands
- White double-satin ribbon, 1½ in. wide

A.

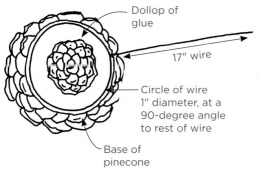

Dollop of glue

17" wire

Circle of wire 1" diameter, at a 90-degree angle to rest of wire

Base of pinecone

DIRECTIONS

1. Fill your bucket about half full with cool tap water. Trim about ½ in. from the bottom of your flower stems; the fresh cuts will encourage the flowers to soak up water to keep them fresh. Place your flowers in the bucket to keep them hydrated until you're ready to assemble the bouquet.

2. First, attach wires to your pinecones. Cut an 18-in. length of floral wire. Hold the cut wire straight up and down. Bend the top of the wire to a 90-degree angle, about 1 in. from the top. Curve that 1-in. segment into a circular shape. This creates a base for the pinecone to sit and some surface area for the glue to attach. On the bottom of one of the pinecones, add a generous dollop of hot glue. Press the curved wire base into the glue and hold it there for a few seconds, until the glue begins to solidify and is able to support the wire **(drawing A)**. Add wires to the remaining cones.

3. Now it's time to put on your DIY florist cap! First, gather your hydrangea stems together in one hand. You'll notice it's already a very full bouquet. At this point you are welcome to trim away some of the outer hydrangea clusters, depending on how full or dramatic you want the bouquet to be.

4. Holding the hydrangea bundle in one hand, insert the roses throughout the bouquet, as evenly spaced and distributed as possible. Symmetry looks great in this bouquet, but it doesn't have to be absolutely perfect.

5. Slip a rubber band or two around the stems to keep the arrangement together. The band should just hold them together but not be tight enough to bend or bruise the stems.

6. Now it's time to add the veronica. These tall flowers look best near the top part of the bouquet. Add a few clusters of stems

around the top third of the arrangement, slipping the stems through the rubber bands to hold them in place.

7. Add the wired pinecones into the mix, distributing them evenly throughout. The wires will allow you to adjust their height and angle. As with the flowers, slip the wires into the rubber bands.

8. Turn the bouquet around and look for any bare spaces or overly packed areas. By moving the flowers around or trimming away extraneous blooms, you can add shape to the bouquet. Look for bruised or damaged blooms; remove them if necessary.

9. Trim the stems to about 1½ times the height of your fist. This should give you plenty of room to hold the bouquet. Snip the pinecone wires with wire cutters.

10. The final step is to wrap the stems with ribbon a few times to cover the rubber bands and to hold the bouquet together. Tie it with a pretty bow and you're set to walk down the aisle!

Price Breakdown

YOUR COST

Hydrangea, 4 stems	$20.00
Roses, ½ dozen	$10.00
Veronica, 1 bunch	$7.50
Hot glue	$4.00
Floral wire	$3.00
Pinecones	$6.00
Ribbon	$4.00
TOTAL	**$54.50**

STORE COST

A florist would typically charge **$100** or more for a similar bouquet style.

tips & hints

- The size of hydrangea varies from vendor to vendor. If you're ordering online, always get an approximate measurement of the head size so you'll know how many to order to fit the scale you need.

- As a general rule, order one-third more flowers than you think you'll need to account for damaged blooms that may occur in shipping or assembly.

- It is of the utmost importance to keep your flowers in water until the very last moment to help keep them fresh and prevent wilting.

- Roses that have had a chance to open a bit look better than tight buds. Order your roses to arrive 2 to 3 days ahead of your production day so they have time to open up.

- Pinecones come in many different species and sizes.

(I used Lodgepole for this project.) You may want to choose a species that's indigenous to your area or find a different size or an unusual color to suit your style.

- There are several pinecone vendors online where you may browse and purchase your perfect cone if you don't have access to free pinecones in your area. (Beware of taking pinecones from federal land; you could end up in big trouble!)

Floating Crystal and Pearl Necklace

"I want my maids to sparkle like a million twinkling stars in a clear midnight sky." My adorable friend Tilden said this while brainstorming over what kind of necklaces we should create to go with her bridesmaids' delicate tulle gowns. "But I don't want it to be over the top."

Tilden is a bit dramatic, sure, but that's part of her charm. Helping her find a demure-with-a-kick accessory was an irresistible challenge. What would make a "wow" statement without being overwhelming, be fashionable and current, and still feel bridesmaid-y?

After knocking out a few prototypes, we decided on an illusion necklace. You've probably seen them before: a row or two of sparkly pearls or crystals suspended on clear wire so that they look like they're "floating" on the wearer's neck. Our twist, to fit Tilden's requirement for something a bit bold, was to use five strands of pearls and crystals for maximum impact.

This is a fantastic beginner's project because it doesn't require many tools or previous jewelry-making experience. The style isn't just for maids, either. You can switch out pearls for gemstones (or faux gemstones) and crystals or other types of beads to make something smashing for your bridal ensemble.

CRAFTY COMMITMENT

2 to 3 hours

SOLO A-GO-GO

This is an afternoon to throw on your earbuds and chill at the kitchen table while listening to your favorite guilty-pleasure playlist. No one has to know you still love '90s boy bands!

SUPPLIES

- Ruler
- Wire cutters
- 1 roll clear beading wire
- Clear tape
- 144 crystals, clear, 4 mm (I used fewer than 10)
- 50 crystals, clear, 6 mm round (I used fewer than 10)
- 100 pearls, white, 4 mm round (I used fewer than 10)
- 100 pearls, light gray, 4 mm round (I used fewer than 10)
- 50 pearls, white, 6 mm round (I used only a couple)
- 144 size 1 tubular crimp beads, silver (I used around 30)
- Crimping tool
- 1 lobster clasp set
- 4 crimp tubes, size 2

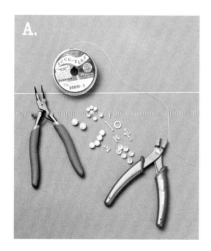

A.

DIRECTIONS

1. Begin by measuring and cutting the wire into five lengths: 25, 23½, 22, 20½, and 18 in. **(photo A)** Lay the wires on a flat surface in order of length, with the longest strand nearest you, and tape one end down on the work surface. Leave about 1 in. of space between each wire to give yourself room to work **(drawing A)**.

2. Next string the pearls, crystals, and crimp beads on the wire strands in the formation that you like. To do so, slip a crimp bead onto the loose end of one of your wire strands, then slide on a pearl, crystal, or a combination thereof, and end with a crimp bead. The crimping beads are small tubes that act as stoppers when they're pressed (or crushed) into place with the crimping tool. You'll need one crimping bead before and after each bead or bead cluster. I recommend placing all of your beads on the wires before you crimp them in place. Once they're set with crimping beads, they often can't be removed.

3. You can be as minimal or as over the top as you like; don't be afraid to play around. It's best to stagger placement on each strand so that the beading doesn't overlap or create unintentionally big clusters. Leave at least 1 in. from each end of wire without adornment so that you have room to add your clasps.

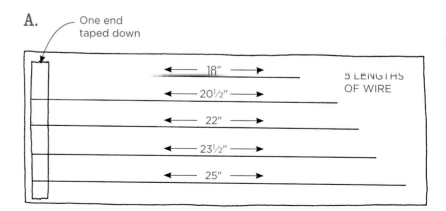

A.   One end taped down

18"
20½"
22"
23½"
25"

5 LENGTHS OF WIRE

B.

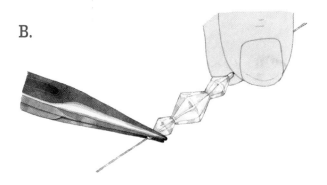

C.

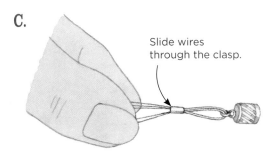

Slide wires through the clasp.

4. Once you've figured out your bead placement, set them in place. Using the crimp tool, press the crimp bead between its teeth and squeeze until it flattens. Repeat for all crimp beads **(drawing B)**.

5. To attach the clasp, thread one end of the three longest wire lengths through a crimp tube and through the loop of a clasp. Thread the wire ends back through the crimp tube. Crimp flat with the bottom portion of a crimping tool. Fold and crimp the tube by using the top portion of the crimping tool. Do the same with the remaining two wire strands. Repeat on the other ends of the wires with the other part of the clasp **(drawing C)**.

tips & hints

- *If you have antique or heirloom jewelry that's broken, this is a great way to repurpose it for your wedding.*

- *It's best to buy in bulk to get the best discounts and to ensure you get enough crystals to finish your project.*

- *Shop around online for the best deals and, if you have time, do order a sample before you commit to buying in bulk. It's hard to know the true color and sparkle factor from Web images.*

- *The necklace can be made of as few or as many strands as you like. The standard necklace length for a single strand is 17 in. Adding 1½ in. to 2 in. between each strand is recommended.*

Price Breakdown

YOUR COST

Wire	**$8.00**
Crystals	**$20.00**
Pearls	**$30.00**
Crimp beads	**$8.00**
Crimping tool	**$10.00**
Clasp set	**$3.00**
Crimp tubes	**$3.00**

TOTAL	**$82.00**

(these supplies will make 2 to 5 necklaces)

STORE COST

A mass-produced, off-the-rack necklace would go for about **$40**. Custom necklaces can run upward of **$100** with higher-end brand-name materials.

CHAPTER FIVE: A Touch of Country

ONE OF THE most popular trends in recent memory is "new country," a mix of heirlooms and modern elements that reinvents tradition with a fun, rustic-chic vibe. Show off your fun and flirty side with a beautiful country bouquet made of crepe paper. Treat your guests to a bit of down-home hospitality with rustic cherry pie favors. Incorporate embroidery, an old-school craft if ever there was one, into a lovely keepsake invitation. Turn an old picture frame into a chic chicken-wire seating card holder. Welcome your guests with a cute hand-painted wedding sign. Country chic: It's old, it's new, and it's something truly special.

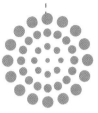

Crepe Paper Bouquet

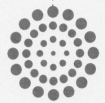

My beloved husband, Jason, swears that one of the exploitation-as-entertainment cable networks is going to film a reality show about me called *Paper Hoarders*. I'm never sure whether he's joking, since I can't see his facial expressions over the stacks of papery goodness crammed into my craft area.

OK, I admit to having a bit of a preoccupation with paper. I've not met beautifully handmade paper from India, a luxe sheet of Crane Lettra, or a fun print from one of my favorite scrapbook companies that I didn't immediately fall for and give a loving home to. Paper is one of the most versatile craft materials that one can buy—and it's usually pretty inexpensive compared to other craft supplies. What's not to love?

One of the latest objects of my paper obsessions is crepe paper: not the thin rolls of streamers that you can pick up at party and craft stores but the high-quality, luxurious crepes coming from Europe. They are, quite frankly, divine for creating beautiful paper crafts.

The European crepes hail mainly from Germany and can be found at a few specialty retailers in the United States (see Resources on page 216 for where to buy). They are much thicker than streamer crepe and come in large

CRAFTY COMMITMENT

10 to 15 minutes per flower

WITH A LITTLE HELP FROM MY FRIENDS

Cutting and assembling hundreds of petals can become quite monotonous if you're going solo. Who wants that? Grab your best gal pals for an afternoon of gossip, cocktails, and camaraderie to make this project a fun memory.

sheets, about 20 in tall by 8 ft. wide. Available in dozens of colors and richly textured, they are perfect for creating beautiful paper flowers and, well, this bouquet. Though the supplies are European, the charm of a handmade paper bouquet is 100 percent country chic.

For this project, I used about 25 flowers. It created a small bouquet, perfect for a petite bride or a bridesmaid or as a toss bouquet. Each flower takes 10 to 15 minutes to complete, including cutting, so allow yourself plenty of time to complete the bouquet. I won't lie to you—assembly can get a bit tedious, so grab a pal to help out and put on some fun music to help pass the time quickly.

SUPPLIES

- Computer with printer
- Petal templates, printed and cut out
- European crepe paper in the colors of your choice, 20-in. by 8-ft. sheets (see Resources on page 216 for retailers)
- Scissors
- 1 spool of floral wire, found at most craft stores, cut to 18-in. lengths
- Floral tape
- Wire cutters
- Straight pins
- Satin ribbon, 1 in. wide

DIRECTIONS

1. Copy and print the petal templates onto regular printer paper. Cut the template shapes from the printed sheet. You'll be using these quite a bit to create the petals for all of your flowers.

2. Unroll a sheet of crepe paper and cut from it a 1½-in. length that's 2 in. tall to create the stamen, or center, of the flower. Along one of the short sides of the paper, make small cuts, ⅛ in. apart and 1½ in. down, along the entire length **(drawing A)**.

3. Next, take one of the 18 in. lengths of wire and fold it down, about 1½ in. from the top. This creates more surface area for the crepe paper fringe you've created to adhere to. Now attach the fringed crepe paper to the wire. Hold one end of the crepe tightly to the wire, about 1½ in. from the top, and wind the crepe around the wire, keeping it taut **(drawing B)**. Secure it in place with a few rounds of floral tape. Do make sure the floral tape touches both

the bottom edge of the crepe paper fringe and the wire so that it stays in place. I recommend doing a bunch of these at a time so that you don't have to interrupt your assembly process after each flower to do this step **(drawing C)**.

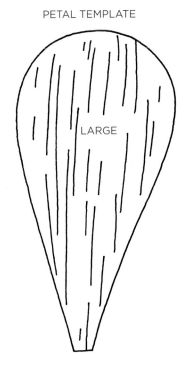

4. Now it's time to start cutting the flower petals. From a crepe paper sheet, cut a 3-in.-tall by 12-in.-wide piece, orienting it so that the pleats or grain of the crepe paper run up and down the 3-in. side. This will be important when you start cutting and shaping the petals; otherwise they'll be misshapen and uneven, making your assembly a hassle.

5. Fold the strip in half and then in half again **(drawing D)**.

6. Place one of the petal templates (either the large or the small) on top of the folded crepe paper and place pins through the template and layers to hold it in place; one or two should be sufficient. The lines on the template should be parallel with the grain of the crepe paper **(drawing E)**.

7. Cut the petal shape from the paper bundle. For each flower, you'll need 7 large petals and 5 small petals, all of the same crepe paper color. You'll notice that you're creating only 4 petals per bundle. You can use longer lengths of 3-in.-tall crepe pieces to create more petals per bundle. Be extra-careful if you do. The crepe paper tends to slide around when you use longer pieces and more folds, which creates uneven cuts. Again, it's best to do the cutting in bulk so that you don't have to stop production to do the cutting for each flower. What can I say? I like efficient production lines.

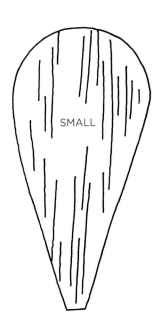

8. Once your petals are cut from the crepe sheets, it's time to give them some character. Right now, you have a ton of petals that are flat, 2-D pieces of paper. Boring! Let's get going and turn them

continued on p. 116

A.

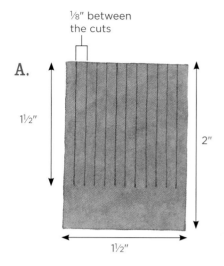

⅛″ between the cuts

1½″

2″

1½″

B.

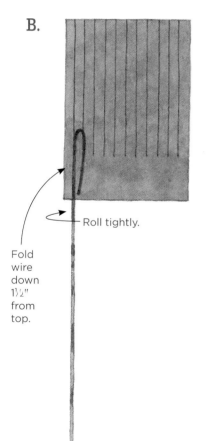

Roll tightly.

Fold wire down 1½″ from top.

into itty-bitty 3-D pieces of art. Holding a petal in both hands, with your thumbs in the center of the petal, gently stretch the crepe outward while pushing gently inward with your thumbs **(drawing F)**. This creates a cup shape like you'd see in a real flower petal. This point is where your diligence with orienting and cutting the petal templates with the grain of the crepe paper will pay off. If your cutting is off, the petals will stretch into strange, wonky shapes. If you encounter uneven cuts, just start fresh with new petals. Trying to salvage uneven petals is often more trouble than it is worth.

9. Pleat the base of each petal by giving it a little pinch. Inner petals may need a double pleat, while the outer petals generally need only a single pleat. Neatness does not count here, so don't worry about perfection! You're just adding a bit more realism to the flower's shape.

10. Finally! It's time to assemble the flower. To attach flower petals to the wire, hold a small petal against the stem so that the top comes just above the stamen. Wrap a piece of floral tape along the bottom of the petal to secure it in place on the wire. Don't worry about buildup of floral tape in the assembly process; it serves to help create the bulb shape of the flower.

11. Continue attaching petals to the wire, starting with the small petals and then moving to the large. The tops of large petals should rise slightly above the smaller petals and overlap slightly as you move around the flower, just as with a real rose or other flower. The petals should be evenly spaced around the flower, but don't feel compelled to achieve absolute perfection. Real flowers are quite unbalanced and riddled with imperfection, yet they're still beautiful **(drawing G)**.

12. Once you've completed your flowers, it's time to put them together into a bouquet. Yay! Gather 3 flower stems and tape them together with floral tape, from the bottom of the flower bulb to about 3 in. down. Now start adding a few flowers at a time, slightly below the first batch, securing them in place with floral tape. Continue to add flowers until you've achieved the fullness you like or until you've used up all of your flowers—whichever suits your fancy.

continued on p. 118

C.

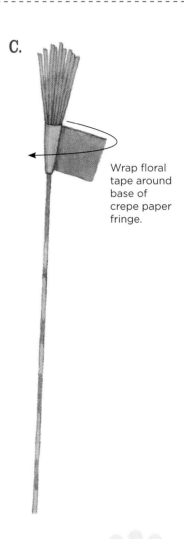

Wrap floral tape around base of crepe paper fringe.

D.

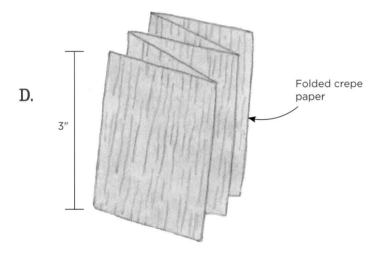

3"

Folded crepe paper

E.

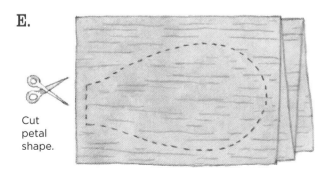

Cut petal shape.

F.

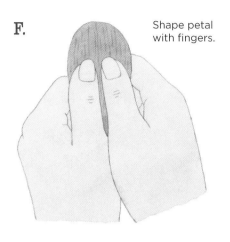

Shape petal with fingers.

13. When your bouquet is full of flowery goodness, go ahead and wrap the entire length of wire in floral tape, making sure to cover the exposed ends of the wire so you don't get poked. Ouch!

14. The finishing touches are to wrap the wire stem with ribbon and to fluff up the flowers. Use a straight pin to secure a length of satin ribbon to the top of the stems, just below the flower heads. Wrap the ribbon tightly around the stems until you reach the end. Pin the ribbon in place and snip the excess ribbon off at an angle. As you've been working, you may have smushed (yes, that's the technical term) the flowers. That's OK. Just use your fingers to stretch and manipulate the outer petals of your flowers to get them to perk up again.

G.

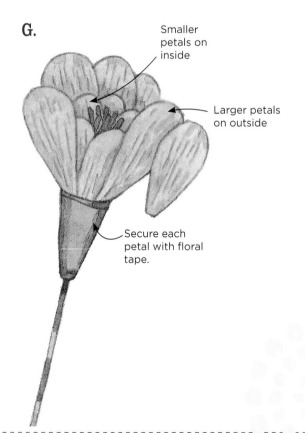

Smaller petals on inside

Larger petals on outside

Secure each petal with floral tape.

Price Breakdown

YOUR COST

Crepe paper (5 sheets, 1 color each)	**$35.00**
Floral wire	**$4.00**
Floral tape	**$3.00**
Ribbon	**$3.00**
TOTAL	**$45.00**

STORE COST

Single crepe paper flowers can cost upward of **$4.00**.

tips & hints

- Crepe paper comes in dozens of colors, sometimes double-sided with different colors on each side. Don't be afraid to experiment with wild or unusual color combinations!

- Crepe paper is very stretchy; it can overstretch, but it takes a lot to get it to that point. Snip off a piece of crepe and play with it before you start creating your flowers to get a feel for how it can be manipulated with stretching and creasing.

- Keep your flowers out of direct sunlight. The dyes in crepe paper fade quite easily.

- Working with floral tape can be maddening sometimes! It's not you. It's the tape. I like working with smaller precut lengths of 4 in to 6 in. rather than trying to cut from a full roll. Cut a bunch of strips before you start assembly so they're ready to go when you begin wrapping petals. It'll make your life much easier.

- Crepe paper streamers from your party store? They are so not the same! You can create flowers in this manner from crepe paper streamers you find at party and craft stores, but you're not going to get the quality and shapes you'll achieve with the higher-end European stuff.

- Floral tape is available in different colors and shades, mostly greens and browns. The green tape is easiest to find and works great for most flowers. The brown is fine, too, and tends to make the floral stems less noticeable when used with darker flowers. Whatever you choose is fine. Don't sweat it too much.

- The templates can be scaled to any size you'd like. Using multiple flower sizes creates a visually stunning bouquet, but it's a lot more work. Do allow yourself plenty of extra time if you introduce more flower sizes to your bouquet.

- The flowers work great in boutonnieres and corsages as well as for cake decorations.

- While the heavy crepe paper is pretty sturdy for use as a bouquet, it is still delicate as far as paper goes. Keep it away from open flame, water, and food.

Mini Cherry Pie Favor

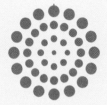

Sure, it looks humble, but the iconic cherry pie holds a legendary allure for connoisseurs of the homemade baking arts. Who could resist sweet yet lightly tart plump cherries with a smooth, succulent filling all held in a rich, flaky crust? Only those with cold, cold hearts, I say.

This precious little pie makes an excellent single-serving favor or an alternative to a wedding cake as part of a dessert buffet. These are super-cute when presented in a muslin bag (with a cello bag around the pie to keep it fresh and lint-free) and a disposable wooden spoon.

The only specialized tool required is a cherry pitter for the fresh cherries. The mini pie tins can be found in grocery stores and restaurant supply shops. Premade pie dough is readily available at warehouse stores in bulk to save you time and frustration if you're piecrust-challenged.

To make your life even easier, the pies can be partially made weeks in advance and frozen until it's time to bake them. Just let the frozen pies thaw to room temperature, then bake according to the directions that follow. It's best to bake these no more than 2 days ahead to help ensure your guests enjoy fresh pies. The directions and recipe for this project make 7 mini pies.

CRAFTY COMMITMENT

60 to 90 minutes per batch of pies

WITH A LITTLE HELP FROM MY FRIENDS

If you have a gaggle of grannies, an abundance of aunties, or feeling-left-out moms, this is the perfect project to get them involved. Create precious family memories while baking some delicious treats for your guests.

SUPPLIES

- 4 Tbs. quick-cooking tapioca
- $\frac{1}{8}$ tsp. salt
- 1 cup sugar
- 4 cups pitted fresh cherries
- $\frac{1}{4}$ tsp. almond extract
- $\frac{1}{2}$ tsp. vanilla extract
- All-purpose flour
- 1 package (15 oz.) frozen piecrust
- Mini pie tins, 3$\frac{1}{2}$ in. in diameter
- 1$\frac{1}{2}$ Tbs. butter

A.

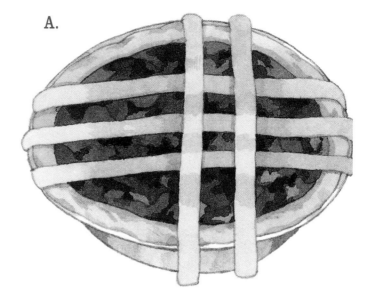

DIRECTIONS

1. In a large bowl, combine the tapioca, salt, sugar, cherries, and almond and vanilla extracts. Let stand for 15 minutes. Lightly dust flour onto your work surface and gently unfold the piecrust onto the surface.

2. Using the top of a 3$\frac{1}{2}$-in. aluminum pie tin as a template, use a knife to cut out 7 rounds, adding $\frac{1}{4}$ in. around each one.

3. Butter each pie tin and place a piecrust round into each pie tin. Fill with cherry filling.

4. Using the piecrust leftovers, cut long, thin strips of dough for the lattice top of the pies.

5. Gently lay the strips over the top of the pies, cutting the excess off of each end and firmly pressing the strips onto the pie tin rim to secure them. Turn the pie 90 degrees and lay strips across the previous ones, again pressing them into the rim to secure **(drawing A)**.

6. Preheat the oven to 375°F. Place the pies on a baking sheet to catch any spills while they bake.

7. Bake the pies for 15 to 20 minutes or according to the recommendations on the piecrust packaging.

8. Allow to cool completely before packaging them up for transportation.

tips & hints

- *If cherry pie isn't your thing, you can use any of your favorite pie fillings for this project.*

- *Cherries are in season during the late summer months. If fresh cherries aren't in season or available in your area, frozen cherries work just as well. Bonus: They're often already pitted for your convenience. Be sure to select unsweetened fruit; otherwise this recipe will be far too sugary.*

- *I love these when presented in muslin or burlap bags. Waxed paper bags are fabulous, too.*

Price Breakdown

YOUR COST

Pie filling ingredients	**$4.00**
Frozen piecrust	**$3.19**
Mini pie tins (8 pack)	**$3.00**

TOTAL   **$10.19**
for 7 pies or
$1.45 each

STORE COST

Individual pies from local bakeries typically cost anywhere from **$2.50** to **$4.00** each.

FIT YOUR STYLE

Having a winter wedding?
Try a yummy pumpkin, apple, or mincemeat pie instead of cherry.

Winnie + Cameron

together with their families
invite you to join them as
they celebrate their wedding
on 18 July, 2013
at 2:30 in the afternoon
at the
Berkeley Botanical Gardens
Berkeley, California

Reception to follow at the
Brazilian Room in Berkeley.

Embroidered Invitation

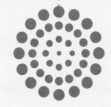

Few things excite my crafty little heart more than being able to take an old craft and find unusual applications for it, like crocheting beautiful, ornate sleeves for vases or using gel-based food colors to rubber-stamp designs on cookies and cakes. This project takes embroidery—once relegated to "Bless This House" samplers—and turns it into a piece of contemporary wedding art by using it on an invitation. Don't worry; this isn't your grandma's embroidery. We're using a more modern floral motif that's befitting a stylish and country chic couple like you.

If you've never picked up a needle and thread, that's OK. This is a project that beginners can master with a little practice beforehand. My only caveat about these invitations is that they are time-consuming. Please do allow yourself plenty of time to complete them, and grab some helping hands to save time and your sanity. You know that this is the kind of project that aunties and grandmas would be delighted to chip in and help with!

CRAFTY COMMITMENT

30 to 45 minutes
per invitation

WITH A LITTLE HELP FROM MY FRIENDS

This is an ideal project
for helping hands
and nimble fingers!
Gather a few sewing-savvy
pals for an afternoon of
embroidery goodness.

SUPPLIES

- Crane Lettra 110-lb. cardstock in Fluorescent White, 8½ in. by 11 in.
- Eggplant-colored cardstock, 8½ in. by 11 in.
- Paper cutter
- Computer with Microsoft Word
- Printer
- Rubber stamp
- Dye-based ink pad to match or coordinate with your floss color
- Piece of thick cardboard or a self-healing cutting mat
- Paper piercing tool, found at craft stores
- Embroidery floss to coordinate with colored cardstock
- Embroidery needle
- Scissors
- Clear single-sided tape
- Double-sided tape

DIRECTIONS

1. Start this project off by cutting the cardstocks to size. With your paper cutter, trim the white cardstock to 5 in. by 7 in. and the eggplant cardstock to 5¼ in. by 7¼ in.

2. Print your invitation wording on the white cardstock, leaving a 3-in. margin on the bottom of the page. This blank area will be where the embroidery goes later on. Note: If your rubber stamp is smaller or larger than 3 in., you will need to adjust your bottom margin accordingly. To set up your invitation for printing, open Microsoft Word and create a new document. From the Page Setup menu, select "Custom Page Size" from the "Settings" options. Set the custom page size for "5" wide by "7." Click "OK." Set the margin spacing to "0.25" for the left and right margins. For the top, set the margin spacing to "0.25." For the bottom, set the spacing to "3.0."

3. Enter your invitation wording. Save the document and print it onto the Crane Lettra cardstock.

4. It's time to get those fingers inky! In this step you'll be adding a rubber-stamped image onto the invitation to serve as a template for your embroidery. To ink a rubber stamp, gently tap it several times on the surface of the ink pad to get the entire rubber image evenly inked. Firmly press the stamp onto the invitation where you'd like the image to go. Don't twist or move the stamp when you press down; you'll smudge the image. Lift the stamp straight off the paper. Voilà! You now have a beautifully stamped image. Set each stamped invite aside to dry as you work. A dye-based ink should dry in minutes.

5. Now you get to start the embroidery process; don't freak out if you've never embroidered. It's just a matter of moving a needle and thread from one hole to another. "What holes?" you ask. The

ones you're going to create right now with that paper piercing tool you just bought. Place the stamped invitation on top of the thick piece of cardboard (like a shipping box) or self-healing cutting mat. You're creating some elevation so that the needle of the piercing tool has space to go all the way through the cardstock. Working your way around the entire outline of the stamped image, poke holes about every ¼ in. Make sure not to get any closer than ⅛ in. to the edges of the cardstock; you'll risk ripping the paper if you do.

6. Next, thread your embroidery needle. Embroidery floss comes in long bundles of 6 strands that are twisted together, called skeins. Unwind 2 long strands of embroidery floss from the skein and

continued on p. 128

Price Breakdown

YOUR COST

Crane Lettra cardstock (25 sheets)	$15.00
Eggplant-colored cardstock	$3.00
Paper piercing tool	$4.00
Embroidery floss	$6.00
Tape	$4.00

TOTAL $32.00
for 50 invitations or
$0.64 each

STORE COST

Embroidered invitations are exceedingly hard to find from stationers due to the amount of work that goes into them; expect to pay **$8.00** to **$12.00** or more for a single invitation.

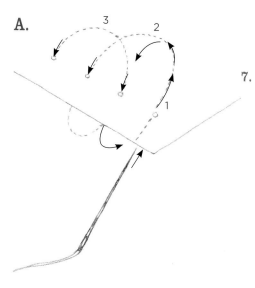

A.

thread them through the embroidery needle. Knot the ends as you would a regular needle and thread. You're ready to get embroidering!

7. Start by picking an area to concentrate on. I like starting from the bottom left and working upward and outward in small sections. You may find your design necessitates that you work differently—that's perfectly OK. This is just a guide. Do what works best for you! Begin by passing the threaded needle from the underside through one of the holes. Next, thread the needle down through the hole next to it. Perfect! The next bit may seem counter-intuitive, but do it anyway. Pass the needle back up through the first hole. What you're doing is called the "backstitch." It creates a solid line of stitching. Move through the remaining holes, using the backstitch technique until you run out of floss or finish an area of the design. At the points where you need to stop and rethread or move to another section, push the needle through a hole so that it's on the bottom side of the card. Snip the floss and use a bit of clear tape to hold the cut floss in place. Rethread your needle and start where you left off **(drawing A)**.

8. Whew! You're just about done! After you've embroidered your invitation, you'll notice the back of the cardstock is a bit of a mess. No worries. That's what the coordinating cardstock is for. You'll be creating a mat with it so that the back side is concealed. Apply strips of double-sided tape to the back of the invitation and firmly press the invitation onto the eggplant-colored cardstock, centering it from top to bottom and from side to side. That's it! Your hand-embroidered masterpiece is ready to send to your nearest and dearest.

tips & hints

- *Crane Lettra cardstock is the crème de la crème of stationery paper. It's thick and luxurious—and a bit pricey. I chose it for this particular project because it holds up well to the piercing and embroidery process. You can use other cardstocks, but they'll need to be 110-lb. weight or higher to really handle this technique.*

- *Embroidery floss is available in hundreds of colors and it's generally very inexpensive. Don't be shy about mixing and matching different shades and hues to suit your unique style.*

- *Paper dulls needles quite rapidly. Have a few extra embroidery needles on hand when you're doing this project. You'll be able to tell the needle is dull when it starts tearing the paper rather than poking right through it.*

- *Rubber stamps come in countless designs, and you can even have custom ones created at office supply stores and online. The best stamps for this project have open, line-drawing type designs. You don't want anything too small or ornate here. You can use text as your template, but again, it needs to be wide enough so that you have enough room to poke holes and thread floss through.*

- *If rubber stamping isn't your thing, no problem! You can use traditional embroidery patterns. Hundreds of thousands are available online in nearly every imaginable style and theme for cheap or free. Feeling adventuresome? Go 100 percent freehand!*

- *Can't find a paper piercing tool? A thick needle, an awl, or a thin nail will do. Raid your tool box!*

Chicken-Wire Seating Card Holder

Now that you've agonized over the ideal seating arrangements for your nearest, dearest, and others, you've got to have a way to let them know where to sit. Behold, the chicken-wire seating card holder.

This beauty of a project perfectly personifies country chic and can be assembled in less than an hour. The 24-in. by 30-in. frame I used held 40 names quite nicely; you'll need a larger frame if your guest list exceeds 40, of course. Or you could opt to have multiple frames of different shapes and sizes displayed in your seating area, which would be so gorgeous!

A word of caution about this project: Chicken wire can cause injury. Be extra-careful when handling and cutting chicken wire; it does puncture and scratch skin. Wear gloves and safety glasses to protect yourself from any harm.

As for finding the perfect frame, I spent weeks at garage sales, flea markets, and secondhand stores in search of a pretty frame to no avail and ended up using a brand-new frame from my favorite mega craft store. Allow yourself plenty of time for your own frame search, as you may run into a drought of frame options like I did.

CRAFTY COMMITMENT

3 hours

CRAFTY COUPLE

Even the most craft-phobic dudes can get on board with this project. Set your guy to the task of working the tools while you get your craft on with the paper projects— or switch it up! Maybe you're the one who's handy-dandy with tools and he's more interested in the paper stuff. Either way, this is a fun project to collaborate on.

SUPPLIES

- Open-back picture frame, 24 in. by 30 in.
- 1 roll of chicken or aviary wire, found at most hardware stores
- Staple gun
- Safety glasses, found at hardware stores
- Hardware or work gloves
- Heavy-duty wire cutters
- Muslin fabric, 1 yd.
- Fabric shears
- Kraft cardstock, $8\frac{1}{2}$ in. by 11 in.
- Paper cutter
- $\frac{1}{4}$-in. standard hole punch
- White gel ink pen, found at craft and stationery stores
- $\frac{5}{8}$-in.-wide ribbon, about 3 in. per seating card

DIRECTIONS

1. If your frame has glass and a cardboard or fiberboard back, remove and recycle them.

2. Lay the frame on a flat work surface, front side facing down.

3. Unroll a few feet of chicken wire and lay it on top of the frame, positioning the edge of the wire about an inch above the frame's opening.

4. Using your handy-dandy staple gun, staple the chicken wire in place along the top edge, making sure the wire pattern is parallel with the orientation of the frame's opening.

5. Now that you have the chicken wire secured, unroll a few more feet. Holding the wire taut, staple it in place down each side of the frame to secure it in place **(drawing A)**. You may need a helper to hold either the frame or the chicken wire steady while you do this. Have bribes of cupcakes or cocktails on hand as a post-work incentive.

6. You've noticed you haven't cut anything yet, right? Don't worry, it's coming up. Continue stapling down the wire until you have come to the bottom of the frame opening. Again, leaving about an inch of overlap from the opening, secure the chicken wire in place along the bottom edge.

7. It's time to cut! Put on your safety glasses and gloves and use the wire cutters to trim away the excess chicken wire around the perimeter of the frame's opening. You'll likely get bits of wire that stick up at this point; it's perfectly OK—and highly recommended— that you staple them down to prevent injury.

A.

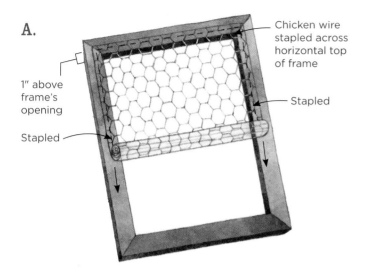

Chicken wire stapled across horizontal top of frame

1" above frame's opening

Stapled

Stapled

B.

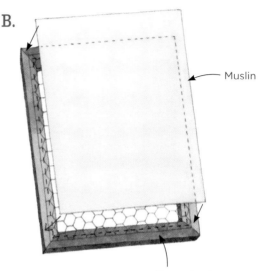

Muslin

Frame back with stapled chicken wire

8. The next step is to cover the back with muslin fabric. This serves as a nice backdrop to your seating cards. Measure out the length and width of the frame's opening and add $1\frac{1}{2}$ in. (You want the fabric to at least cover the wire on the back of the frame, but it needn't cover the entire frame back.) Staple it in place as you did the chicken wire; holding the fabric taut as you secure it to the frame **(drawing B)**. Flip the frame over and admire your mad stapling skills!

9. Now it's time to create those pretty little seating cards. Cut $1\frac{3}{8}$-in. by 3-in. strips of kraft cardstock.

10. Holding the cardstock with the short side facing up, punch a centered hole with the $\frac{1}{4}$-in. hole punch, about $\frac{1}{4}$ in. down from the top. This is where your ribbon will eventually secure the card to the wire. *continued on p. 134*

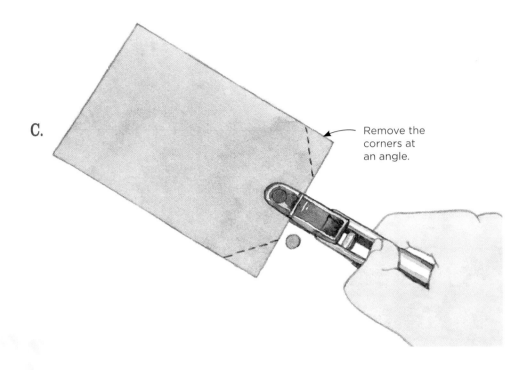

C.

Remove the corners at an angle.

11. Now, this seems a little tricky, but using the ¼-in. hole punch, take little ticket stub–style bites out of the top corners of the seating cards. Slide the cardstock about one-quarter of the way into the punch and punch the card **(drawing C)**. Repeat for all of your cards.

12. You're almost done! With the gel pen (one of my favorite stationery products, ever), write the names and the table numbers of your guests on each card. Set them aside to dry; sometimes gel inks take a while before they're smudge-proof.

13. The final step is to secure the cards to the chicken wire with the ribbon. Simply thread the ribbon through the seating-card hole and then through one of the loops of the chicken wire. Tie it with a simple knot or a pretty bow and you're good to go!

tips & hints

- *Hardware stores usually carry chicken wire and/or aviary wire. Aviary wire has smaller openings in the wire than chicken wire. Both work well for this project. If you're using smaller frames or want to squeeze in more cards on a frame, go with aviary wire.*

- *Big box craft stores carry open-backed frames that are typically cheaper than regular picture frames.*

- *If you're lucky enough to have an IKEA nearby, do check their frame and picture department. While their selection is typically modern in style, they occasionally have fun, ornate frames that are inexpensive.*

- *Secondhand stores, flea markets, garage sales, and household discount stores are great places to find frames. Look for old mirrors as well as picture frames for unique pieces that can be repurposed for this project.*

- *Don't be afraid to alter a frame! A whitewash would be utterly gorgeous for a country wedding, or try some distressing with sandpaper for a more rustic look.*

- *Any fabric can be used to back the wire. I chose muslin because it's simple, theme-appropriate, and cheap. Gingham, subtle country prints, an old quilt, or denim would all be quirky but pretty substitutes.*

Price Breakdown

YOUR COST

Frame	$30.00
Chicken wire	$13.00
Fabric	$4.00
Cardstock	$2.00
Hole punch	$1.00
Ribbon	$5.00
TOTAL	**$55.00**

STORE COST

Custom seating charts can cost more than **$125.00** from specialty designers.

Wooden Wedding Sign

My one concession to reality TV is the type of show where the hosts go scrounging through abandoned attics, creepy basements, and dilapidated sheds in the hopes of finding rare treasures or, at least, cool knickknacks. Whenever they come up, triumphant, with vintage signage, I get a little excited. I love old hand-painted signs. They're quirky and fun and oftentimes really beautiful pieces of period artwork. Not only would they look fabulous in my home, but they'd also be ideal for displaying at weddings.

Unfortunately, real vintage signs can cost thousands of dollars, which makes them out of the question for wedding decor. However, creating one's own sign is a pretty swell idea. Not only can you use it to add a whimsical touch to your wedding, but you can also have a neat memento of your wedding day to display in your home for years to come.

CRAFTY COMMITMENT

2 to 3 days

SOLO A-GO-GO

The work of this project is done in mostly small chunks of time with long waits for drying time, so take advantage of time in between errands and obligations to grab some quiet time for yourself.

SUPPLIES

- 1 piece of ½-in.-thick plywood, 18 in. by 48 in.
- 120-grit (or finer) sandpaper
- Old towel or rag
- Newspaper
- Soft bristle brush or lint-free cloths for applying stain
- Water-based wood stain
- Pencil
- Printout or graphic (optional)
- Graphite transfer paper (optional)
- Yardstick
- Paint brushes, 1 in. to 2 in. wide
- Paint pens for detail work
- Acrylic paint, assorted colors
- Paper plate
- Spray sealer

DIRECTIONS

1. If you love working outside, you're going to love this project! Grab some lemonade, throw on your sunglasses, and get craftin'. To kick things off, you'll need to prep the plywood for staining. Use a piece of sandpaper to sand down the surface and edges of the plywood to remove any rough bits. It's important to sand with the grain of the wood, not against it. The smoother the surface, the easier it'll be when it comes time to apply your design.

2. Once you're satisfied with your sanding work, wipe away the dust and debris with an old cloth or rag. Set your sanded board over newspaper. Now it's time to apply the stain.

3. Staining is pretty straightforward. Dip either your brush or a stain cloth into the stain. Apply the stain to the wood in long, even strokes, going with the grain, being careful not to drip or puddle stain in any area. Make sure the surface is evenly covered (be sure to do the edges in this stage), then allow the stain to dry according to manufacturer's recommendations. Flip the board over and finish up the other side. Add a second coat and, if needed, a third, allowing each coat to dry before moving on to the next. Stain really stinks, so do this outside or, if that isn't an option, in a garage or workroom, but please be sure it's a well-ventilated space.

4. So now your beautiful board is stained and ready for adornment. Whip out your pencil and sketch out your wording and graphics. Use a yardstick or straight edge to keep lines level. If you're not comfortable with going freehand, that's OK. You can type out any text you want to put on your sign and either print it in an extra-large font size or take the document (don't forget to bring along the fonts) to a copy center and have it enlarged to the size of your board. If you go this route, you'll need to use graphite copy paper to trace the design from your printout to the board. Spend as much time as you need on this step! When you're working in

pencil, it's easy to fix mistakes or make changes. Do be sure to step away from time to time and evaluate how the sign will look from afar. Is your font big enough to be legible from 10 feet away, or do guests need to be just a few feet away to read it?

5. Satisfied with your rocking design? Let's paint! My strong recommendation is to paint from the top downward. There's nothing worse than leaning over a part of just-painted signage and smearing it with your shirt hem or a wayward elbow. One of my favorite tricks, especially with text, is to use a paint pen in matching colors to your design to outline text and details. It helps set boundaries when coloring in with paint brushes so that your paint doesn't bleed.

6. Dip a small brush into a generous dollop of paint on a paper plate. Wipe away excess on the edge of the plate, then apply the paint to your design. Allow the paint to completely dry before adding another coat if needed.

7. When all is done to your satisfaction, spray your design with a coat of sealer and allow it to dry. You're ready to display your masterpiece!

Price Breakdown

YOUR COST

Plywood	$18.00
Stain	$8.00
Transfer paper	$6.00
Brushes	$8.00
Acrylic paint	$8.00
Spray sealer	$8.00
TOTAL	**$56.00**

STORE COST
Custom-designed wedding signs can cost upward of **$125.00** from specialty graphic designers.

FIT YOUR STYLE

Add sea motifs for a beach or tropical wedding or a cute rendition of a local landmark if you're a city couple.

tips & hints

- This project can be made to any size you want. Most home improvement stores will cut plywood to your dimensions for a nominal fee. Just ask!

- Plywood comes in different thicknesses; I like 1/2 in. because it's sturdy. You could probably get away with 1/4-in. thickness if 1/2 in. seems too heavy to you.

- If the thought of tracing a design bums you out, try a plastic stencil to add a beautiful design element. They can be found in a tremendous array of styles and designs at craft stores and online stencil shops.

- Acrylic paints come in dozens of colors, including metallics. Don't be afraid to play with color.

- Be sure to use water-based stains. Oil-based stains don't play nicely with acrylic paints.

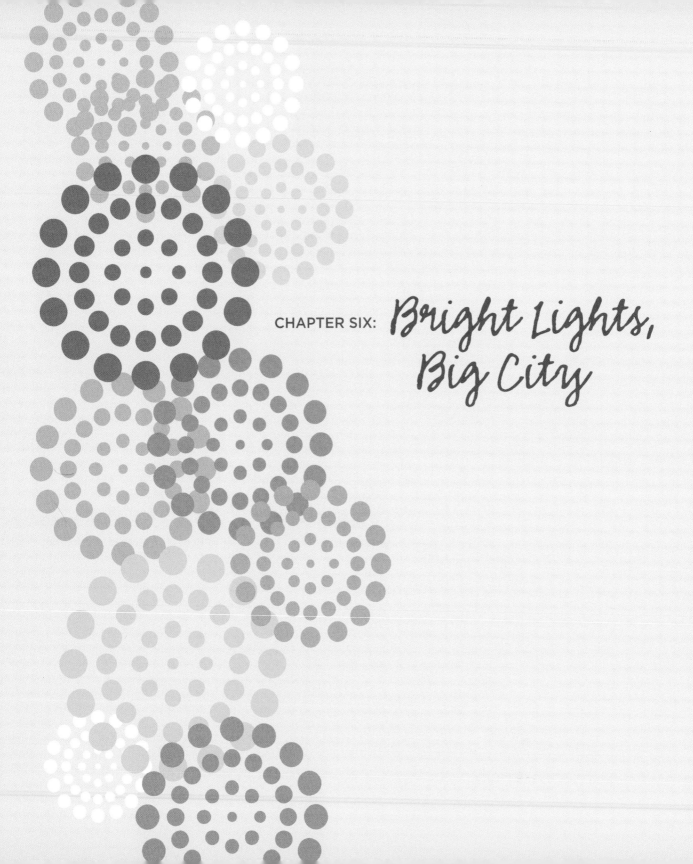

CHAPTER SIX: *Bright Lights, Big City*

CITY DWELLERS or those of you who want to pay homage to the landmarks and quirky places that help define the soul of your favorite city will find inspiration in this chapter. Whether you live in a big city or just love your hometown, let DIY Bride show you how to inject a bit of home-grown love into your wedding theme. Put lady luck on your guests' side with fun scratch-off seating cards. Highlight your favorite subway stops with a crafty program. Get in touch with your Southern roots with a vinyl LP–inspired invitation that celebrates the birthplace of rock 'n' roll, Memphis. Mark your drink station with a New Orleans street sign–inspired plaque. Turn a gorgeous skyline or silhouette of a building into a lighted box to hold your cards at the wedding. All of these projects can be adapted to your own city with just a few changes. Sweet!

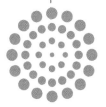

Lewis, Aaron
DeLoise, Camille
Schuyler, Annabeth
Rogers, Liam
A ♥
Berkheiser, Bob
Scratch off the red square below to reveal your VIP seat assignment.
You are seated at lucky table:
A ♦
Marchande, Emile
Scratch off the red square below to reveal your VIP seat assignment.
You are seated at lucky table:
A ♥
Adams, Clive
Scratch off the red square below to reveal your VIP seat assignment.
You are seated at lucky table:
10

Las Vegas Scratch-Off Escort Card

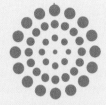

The oh-so-humble seating card is but an afterthought at most weddings. But not at yours, my fun-loving friends. Not just any seating card will do. You've got a style all your own, and delighting in little details is so your thing. Your seating cards need something a bit unexpected, something, perhaps, that gives a nod to the games of chance that Sin City has to offer. Lady luck is on your side with this scratch-off seating card that's sure to delight your crowd of lighthearted and fun-loving guests.

This playing-card-themed seating card features a glittery scratch-off area that reveals the guests' table number. It's a bit Las Vegas glitz, a bit kitsch, and a whole lotta fun. All you need is an Elvis impersonator, some Rat Pack tunes, and a tour of the Strip in a vintage Cadillac to round out your Vegas fantasy wedding.

These scratch-off cards are a lot of fun to make, but beware of the glitter. It's messy! Do the glitter step outside; otherwise your home will sparkle like a Vegas showgirl for months afterward. You'll also need plenty of time to allow the scratch-off solution to dry, at least 24 hours, so start well in advance of your wedding day to avoid any additional stress.

CRAFTY COMMITMENT

3 hours over 2 days

WITH A LITTLE HELP FROM MY FRIENDS

To speed things along, gather a few friends to help with the cutting and assembly. Sweeten the deal with lunch and some Rat Pack music in the background.

SUPPLIES

- Red cardstock,
  $8\frac{1}{2}$ in. by 11 in.

- Black cardstock,
  $8\frac{1}{2}$ in by 11 in.

- White cardstock,
  $8\frac{1}{2}$ in. by 11 in.

- Paper cutter

- Dishwashing liquid

- Silver or other metallic-
  colored acrylic paint

- Paint brush

- Transparency sheets,
  available at office
  supply stores

- Red glitter

- Computer with
  Microsoft Word

- Hoyle Playing Card font
  (a free download from
  www.dafont.com)

- Printer

- Bone folder

- Corner rounder
  paper punch

- Double-sided tape

- Square paper punch, 1 in.

- Spray adhesive

DIRECTIONS

1. For each seating card, you'll need one piece of each color of cardstock cut as follows:
   - Red: $4\frac{1}{4}$ in. by 11 in.
   - Black: $3\frac{1}{4}$ in. by $5\frac{1}{4}$ in.
   - White: 3 in. by 5 in.

   Set them aside while you move on to creating the scratch-off stickers.

2. On a paper plate or in a small mixing bowl, combine 1 part dishwashing liquid to 3 parts acrylic paint. Stir gently (otherwise you'll create a frothy mess) until they're well mixed.

3. Using a paint brush, paint a transparency sheet with the dishwashing-paint mixture in a single, even coat. Sprinkle a generous amount of glitter over the painted area and allow the whole thing to dry completely, about 24 hours. While the scratch-off sheet is drying, get started on your playing card fronts.

4. Install the Hoyle® Playing Card font on your computer, which contains the standard playing card symbols (heart, diamond, club, and spade). Dafont has excellent instructions for font installation on a number of different operating systems in case you need assistance (you can also find this font at other online font sites).

5. Open Microsoft Word and create a new document.

6. From the Page Setup menu, select "Custom Page Size" from the "Settings" options. Set the custom page size for "3" wide by "5." Click "OK."

7. Set the margin spacing to "0.25" for the left and right margins. For the top and bottom, set the margin spacing to "0.25."

8. On the first line of the document, type a letter such as "A" for "ace" and use one of the playing card font symbols, such as a diamond in the color of your choice. Press "enter" twice to move down two lines, and enter the name of a guest.

FIT YOUR STYLE

How about using pink glitter for a fairy-tale wedding?

9. Press "enter" two more times and type in a message of instruction to your guest of what to do with the scratch-off, such as "Scratch off the red square below to reveal your VIP seat assignment." Hit "enter" a few more times and type in "You are seated at lucky table:" Hit "enter" again and, in a larger, bold font, enter the table number your guest will be seated at.

10. Highlight the guest's name, the instructions, and seating number and center them using the alignment button on your Word toolbar.

11. To finish off the card, press "enter" two more times and retype the letter and symbol you used on the first line. Highlight them and align them to the right of the page using the alignment button on the toolbar.

12. Save and print your document on the precut 3-in. by 5-in. white cardstock. Do this for each seating card you wish to create. You're almost done! Hang in there; you're about to start the final assembly.

13. Using the bone folder, crease and fold the 4¼-in. by 11-in. red cardstock in half. This is the base of the seating card; it will be tented so it stands up on the table when complete.

continued on p. 146

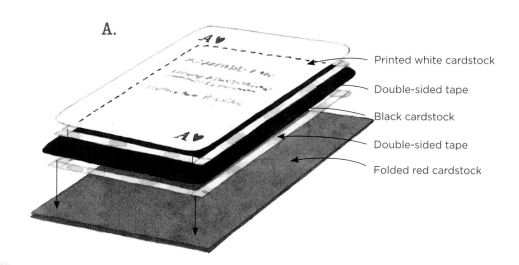

A.

Printed white cardstock

Double-sided tape

Black cardstock

Double-sided tape

Folded red cardstock

14. Next, punch all four corners of the black and white cardstock with the rounded corner punch.

15. It's assembly time! Apply small strips of double-sided tape on the back of the printed white cardstock and adhere that to the front of the black cardstock, centering it from top to bottom and from left to right.

16. Now take the black and white stack and adhere it to the front of the folded red cardstock with double-sided tape, again centering it on the page **(drawing A)**.

17. To finish off the seating card, you'll need to create the little scratch-off squares to adhere over the guests' table assignment. Using the square punch, gently punch out squares from the glittered transparency sheets. Apply the squares to the card face using spray adhesive. It's best to line up a bunch of squares on scratch paper, unglittered sides facing up, and spray them all at once. Press the glittered squares on top of the cards and, voilà, you're done.

tips & hints

- *Not into glitter? That's totally cool. This project can be done without it. The metallic paint and dishwashing liquid solution can be used on its own. Use metallic silver paint for a more traditional lottery or scratch-off vibe.*

- *Any color of glitter can be used. I recommend fine-grade glitters, not chunky ones, for best results. Check out Martha Stewart's line of craft glitters for the best selection on the market.*

- *Don't be afraid to experiment with different fonts, colors, and sizes! What I provide is just a guideline and jumping-off point for your own creativity.*

- *Spray glue should be used outdoors or in an area with excellent ventilation. It is quite possible to get a "contact high" from it, so be careful!*

- *Spray glue is used for the transparency sheets because it dries clear. There are special "vellum" adhesives on the market that produce similar but not-quite-as-good results, and they're generally more expensive. If you want a nonaerosol and nontoxic option to spray adhesive, vellum is it.*

- *Don't forget to have a bunch of coins on hand at the reception for your guests to use to scratch off the squares! Poker chips work great, and you can get them customized with your names and wedding date from online retailers.*

Price Breakdown

YOUR COST

Cardstock	$30.00
Acrylic paint	$1.00
Transparencies	$8.00
Glitter	$5.00
Punches	$15.00
Double-sided tape	$4.00
Spray adhesive	$8.00
TOTAL	**$71.00**

for 100 seating cards
or **$0.71** each

STORE COST

Custom stationers typically charge **$1.50** for a single seating card.

New York Subway Map Wrap Program

The New York subway system not only transports millions of people per day, but it's also been the catalyst for many a romance. Our family friends Caterina and Mario, then-NYU students, met on the subway and fully credit the train ride from Brooklyn to campus as the start of their NYC-fueled love affair.

When Mario and Cat decided to get married, they wanted to give a big old shout-out to where it all started, the subway. Incorporating a subway map and a monogram that gives a slight nod to the train icons is a simple way to add big-city flavor without going full-out with a transportation theme.

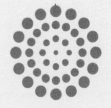

CRAFTY COMMITMENT

3 hours

WITH A LITTLE HELP FROM MY FRIENDS

To speed things along, gather a few friends to help with the cutting and assembly. Sweeten the deal with lunch and some Lady Gaga, Frank Sinatra, or Black Eyed Peas in the background.

SUPPLIES

- Computer with Microsoft Word
- Printer
- 3 pieces of white cardstock, cut to 4 in. by 5½ in.
- 1 sheet of white cardstock, 8½ in. by 11 in.
- Paper cutter or scissors
- Double-sided tape
- 1 printout of the NYC transit map or other city map, 8½ in. by 11 in.

DIRECTIONS

1. To create the printed program, open Microsoft Word and create a new document. From the Page Setup menu, select "Custom Page Size" from the "Settings" options. Set the custom page size for "4" wide by "5.50" high. Click "OK." Set the margin spacing to "0.25" for the left and right margins. For the top and bottom, set the margin spacing to "0.25."

2. To create the subway monogram, select the circle shape from the Basic Shapes tab of the Drawing toolbar in Word. Clicking on the page, drag the mouse until you get the desired size and then drag and drop it into location. To change the default color, double-click on the circle and a format window will appear. Select your color from the drop-down section. Make two circles, one for each partner, each with its own color. Drag the second circle to slightly overlap the first. Double-click it to bring up the formatting box. Change the transparency and fill to 10 percent so that the bottom circle shows through the top circle. It's a neat designer trick.

3. Now, to insert each partner's initial into the circles, click the Text Area box on the Drawing toolbar. Next, click on one of the circles and drag the text box to be the same size as the circle. You may now type inside the circle to insert your favorite font and coordinating font color from the Formatting Palette. Repeat on the other circle. Save your document!

4. Your subway-inspired header is finished! Next, insert your program wording. With paper this small, choose easy-to-read fonts and a font size no smaller than 9 point as a general rule. (Do a test print of your design before committing to a font or font size to make sure it's legible.)

5. When you're satisfied, go ahead and print your program on the 4-in. by 5½-in. cardstock. Set the prints aside until it's time to assemble the final product.

Price Breakdown

YOUR COST

Cardstock	**$60.00**
Double-sided tape	**$9.00**

TOTAL	**$69.00**
	for 100 programs or
	$0.69 each

STORE COST

Custom-designed programs can cost upward of **$3.00** each from wedding stationers.

6. Cut the piece of 8½-in. by 11-in. cardstock in half. You'll end up with two pieces of cardstock 8½ in. wide by 5½ in. tall. Score both pieces of cardstock in half (4¼ in. from either side).

7. Using your paper cutter, cut one side of the scored cardstock diagonally from the top of the score to the bottom corner. Repeat, in reverse, on the second piece of cardstock **(drawing A)** and **(photo A)**.

8. Now it's time to put the pieces together. On the back of the first piece of cardstock, apply a generous amount of double-sided tape. Press the back of this to the front of its companion piece of cardstock to adhere them together. The pieces will overlap to form a single piece that has a triangular piece extending from either side. Fold the triangular flaps into place **(drawing B)**.

9. Cut two triangles from the map printouts. Use the discards from the cards you just cut as templates. Adhere these on top of the triangular flaps on the program pocketfold with the tape.

10. Add a small piece of tape to the back of the top triangle to adhere it to the bottom one. This will secure it in place so that it holds the program. Insert your program printouts.

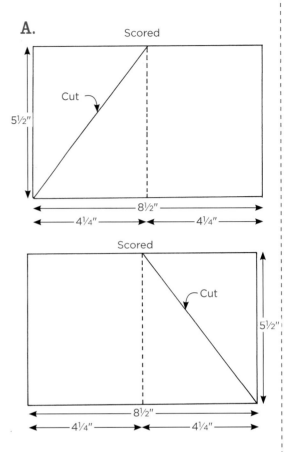

A.

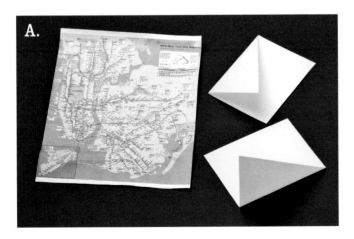

A.

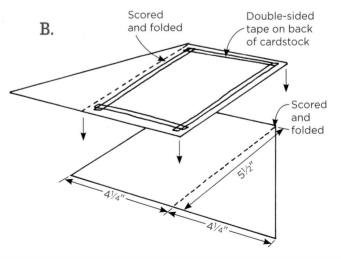

B.

Memphis Invitation

From their fully restored 1952 Cadillac Coupe de Ville right down to their retro-filled mod home, my pals Millie and Steve might seem like they were born in the wrong decade. Looks are deceiving, of course. Steve and Millie are ultra-plugged-in tech nerds who have their fingers on the pulse of all things modern and trendy. They love vintage kitsch, but they're firmly rooted in right now.

When it came time to put together a swell invitation to their old-school Memphis wedding, we pulled together their two loves: the digital world and their to-die-for collection of original vinyl pressings of the best of Sun Records (home of rockabilly and blues legends) recordings. We used a graphic inspired by the logo on their old Sun records and put that on an off-the-shelf CD that's made to look like a vinyl record. The result is a thoroughly modern digital wedding invitation that holds all of the wedding details for the guests packaged in something that looks like a blast from the past.

This project requires Adobe Photoshop™, and the instructions are specific to version CS5 for the Mac. Other versions and even other image/graphic design software will work, but these instructions won't reflect the different processes and functions of other software. Adobe does

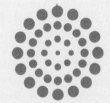

CRAFTY COMMITMENT

3 hours

CRAFTY COUPLE

Even the least crafty guy can get on board with this project. Grab your guy and set him to the task of cutting and labeling while you both listen to your favorite Memphis-inspired playlist.

offer a free 30-day trial of its Photoshop software. Take advantage of the trial period!

The record CD cover we used for this project can be downloaded from www.diybride.com. If that's not to your liking, you can create your own from your favorite vinyl record label by scanning it into your computer and using a graphics program to modify the original to something that fits your style.

SUPPLIES

- Computer with Adobe Photoshop or Photoshop Elements™
- Printer
- Inkjet-compatible label sheets, 8½ in. by 11 in.
- Scissors
- Verbatim Digital Vinyl CD-Rs

DIRECTIONS

1. Open the Disc Label Template in Photoshop. With your mouse, click the Horizontal Type Tool from the Formatting Palette.

2. Click on the Disc Label Template, roughly where you'd like to input the text, in this case the couple's names. Type in the names. Change the font and size to suit your style.

3. Highlight the text with your mouse. From the toolbar, select the Warp Text button. A drop-down menu will appear. Select "Arc" from the Style options. Click "OK."

4. Click the text again to highlight it and use your mouse to drag and drop into position on the template.

5. Your creativity will come into play in this step. Depending on the font size, the number of characters, and the style of your design, you'll likely need to do some alterations at this point. You may need to resize your text or add more curvature to the design (or both) to get it to wrap around the label. For more curvature, select your text and go back to the Warp Text Button. There's a

slider that will allow you to add more or decrease the bend to the text. Just drag the slider button and move it to the "+" side for more or the "−" side for less.

6. The hardest part is done! Now you'll be able to add more text on the template if you'd like. In addition to the couple's names, you could add a wedding date, a location, and the words "invite you to their wedding." Wherever you'd like to add text, just select the type tool from the Formatting Palette, click the mouse on the area, and type.

7. Save your label and print it onto the sticker/label paper.

8. Using scissors, carefully cut out the label. Peel off the backing and stick it to the front of the CD. It's ready for you to add a PDF copy of your invitation, helpful travel and hotel information for your out-of-town loved ones, and other fanciful details to send to your lucky guests!

Price Breakdown

YOUR COST

Label paper	**$8.00**
CDs	**$12.00**

TOTAL	**$20.00**
	for 25 invitations or
	$0.80 each

STORE COST

Custom CD invitations can cost **$5.00** or more per invite from custom stationers.

---

tips & hints

- If Photoshop is out of your budget, don't fret! Adobe offers Photoshop Elements, a lower-end version of Photoshop that has many of the same features, for around $100.00. Still too expensive? Try GIMP, a free open-source digital manipulation program that's available on both Mac and PC platforms.

- Browse the record section at Goodwill or other secondhand stores for awesome inspiration. There are some gems to be found for less than a dollar in many bins. (Old vinyl records make great wedding decorations, too!)

- Looking for killer fonts to add to your clever design? Check out www.dafont.com and www.fontsquirrel.com for excellent free fonts.

- The vinyl-looking CDs can be found in bulk through online retailers. Some will cut you a deal if you order in quantities of 100 or more.

- Stumped for what to put on that CD? Include a PDF of your invitation, hotel and guest information, maps, timelines and schedules, your engagement shots, or even a small movie announcing your engagement.

New Orleans Drink Station

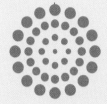

Back in the olden days—the early 1990s, to be exact—I lived in New Orleans while attending college. My love of the Crescent City goes beyond Bourbon Street, beyond the tourist destinations. It extends into the bayous, the little-known neighborhoods, and to the real charm and soul of the city, its people. Though I'm happy to be a Californian, I do miss N'awlins something fierce at times.

When a city grabs you, when you connect with it on a deep and personal level, it can become the basis for your wedding theme. It doesn't have to be all-out all-things-related-to-the-city decor. It can be incorporating little elements that make that city special or identifiable. For me, New Orleans, especially in the French Quarter, has the prettiest street signs. Adapting the iconic street sign as the marker for a cocktail station seemed like the perfect, simple homage to my favorite southern city.

This project is ideal for entry-level crafters. It does take some time to complete, as you'll have to wait for multiple coats of chalkboard paint to dry, so start well in advance of your wedding day so as to not to be rushed. Easily adaptable to other cities, it's a simple craft that's functional and decorative. Gotta love that!

CRAFTY COMMITMENT

24 to 48 hours

SOLO A-GO-GO

Because you'll have extended drying times with the paint, allow yourself a full weekend or a few weeknight evenings to complete the sign. It'll take only a few minutes per session, but with a lot of waiting time in between.

SUPPLIES

- Newspaper

- Unfinished curved wood plaque, 14 in. by 6 in., found at craft stores

- 1 small can of black chalkboard paint, available at craft and hardware stores

- Foam paint brushes

- White paint pens, found at craft stores

- Chalk

- A picture easel, about 18 in. tall and wide enough to accommodate the sign

DIRECTIONS

1. Line your work table with old newspaper to protect its surface.

2. Set the plaque face up on the newspaper. Open the can of paint (read the label to see if it needs to be stirred before use; most chalkboard paint doesn't) and dip your brush in.

3. In thin, even coats, paint the front of the plaque. This feels too easy, doesn't it? Allow the paint to dry per the manufacturer's recommendations. You'll likely need 3 to 5 coats of paint to get good coverage. Allow each coat to dry completely before moving on to the next. Be sure to paint the sides!

4. Once the front is fully painted and is dry, flip it over and paint the back. One or two coats should be sufficient, just enough to cover the exposed wood. Allow it to dry.

5. Flip the plaque over so that the front is facing up again. Now here's where your creativity comes into play! Using the white paint pen, draw a thin, even line around the perimeter of the sign, as close to the edge as possible. Allow the paint to completely dry. You don't want smudges!

6. About an inch from the top, write in your favorite street name or historical site with the paint pen. For that extra nod to New Orleans, add the city's symbol, the fleur-de-lis, at the top. Allow it to dry completely.

7. The last step is to write, in chalk, the names of your signature drinks or cocktails. Set the sign into the cradle of the easel, display, and enjoy!

tips & hints

- *Wood plaques come in a variety of shapes and sizes. If a street sign isn't your thing, it should be easy to find another shape that fits your needs at your local craft store.*

- *Picture easels can be found at craft stores in the framing department. A well-stocked craft store should have several different styles and sizes on the shelves. If not, they're easily found online.*

- *Chalkboard paint is now available in a rainbow of colors! If basic black or old-school green isn't your thing, you can pick up fashionable and bright colors at your local craft and hardware stores. Even more are available from specialty retailers online.*

- *Paint pens come in several colors, too, including brights and metallics.*

- *Fun alternatives to street names would be city landmarks, subway or train stops, names of your college's dorms, your favorite cities, local parks, and points of interest.*

- *Don't be afraid to embellish the design! Stencils are an easy way to add decorative elements, or be daring and go freehand.*

- *Big box craft chains often offer 25 percent to 40 percent discount coupons throughout the year. Don't be shy about taking advantage of those coupons when buying the supplies for this project to save some cash.*

Price Breakdown

YOUR COST

Plaque	$14.00
Paint	$6.00
Brushes	$1.00
Easel	$8.00
TOTAL	**$29.00**

STORE COST

I haven't seen custom drink station signs on the market.

Illuminated Seattle Skyline Card Box

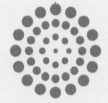

Few things strike fear into the hearts of gift table attendants and newlyweds like a lost or misplaced card at a wedding. Though most guests will send gifts via your registry before or directly after the ceremony, there will be plenty of people who bring cards (many laden with cash, checks, and gift cards) to the ceremony. With piles of gifts and tons of foot traffic, it's easy for small cards to get lost or mixed up with another person's gift. (Imagine the horror Aunt Jean will experience if she's thanked for a bathroom mat instead of that generous $500 gift card to Pottery Barn!)

Most couples employ some sort of gift card basket or a pretty box to catch the cards and extra-small gifts. There's nothing wrong with those options, of course, but why not do something a little unexpected and fun?

Let's take that humble box and create a lighted cityscape on the front! Behind the pop-out skyline are small, powerful LED lights that shine through punched-out holes in the black cardstock. It's a great little project that will make your guests smile and keep your bountiful wedding loot safe and sound.

CRAFTY COMMITMENT

3 hours

SOLO A-GO-GO

Because you'll have extended drying times with the paint, allow yourself a full day to complete your box. This is a good project to get some aggression out: Punching holes is fun and cathartic!

SUPPLIES

- 1 plain shipping box, 13 in. wide by 10 in. tall by 13 in. long
- Box cutter
- Black acrylic paint
- Foam paint brush, 2 in. wide
- Printout of your skyline or landmark
- Black cardstock, 13 in. by 8 in.
- White transfer paper, found at office supply and craft stores
- Pencil
- Hollow hole punch die, 1/4 in. diameter, found at hobby and home improvement stores
- Hammer
- Old cardboard to protect your work surface
- 1 string of battery-powered LED Christmas lights
- Tape
- Double-sided foam tape

DIRECTIONS

1. Seal the shipping box closed. Cut a hole in the top of the box, about 3 in. tall by 5 in. wide, wide enough to accept most standard cards. Save the scrap cardboard for a later step. Paint the box with black acrylic paint, using the foam brush. Allow it to dry.

2. Trace the skyline print out onto the black piece of cardstock by placing the white transfer paper between the paper and the printout. Use your pencil to firmly trace over the details of the printout, making sure to mark where you want the windows or other areas where the light will shine through.

3. Cut the skyline outline from the black cardstock. With the hole punch die and a hammer, punch the windows from the cardstock. It's just like hammering a nail. Place the die over the area where you want to put a hole. Hit the end of the die with a hammer and presto, instant hole. Be sure to have a protected surface (like an old piece of cardboard) behind the paper so that you don't punch straight through to your table or desk **(drawing A)**!

4. Flip the punched skyline over. Wind the lights around the back side of the cutout, place the lights near the holes. Use regular tape to hold them in place. Leave about 6 in. from the last light

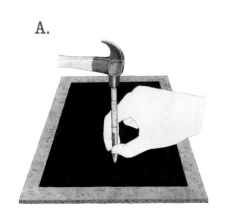

A.

B.

Strand of mini lights near holes

Wire held down by tape

Cardstock back

that is secured to the power source unsecured so that you can run the power source inside of the box to hide it **(drawing B)**.

5. On the front of the box, about 1 in. from the bottom, and centered from left to right, cut a 2-in. by 1-in. hole. This is where you'll put the power supply through during the final assembly so that it's hidden from sight.

6. Cut 8 pieces, about 1 in. square, from the scrap cardboard. Stick two pieces together with double-sided foam tape. Repeat for the other 6 pieces so that you have 4 stacks. With double-sided foam tape, stick one stack at each corner (or nearest a corner) of your cutout. Don't remove the backing yet!

7. To set up the card box for display, line up the bottom of the skyline with the bottom of the box. Turn on the power supply and slip it through the hole in the front of the box. Remove the backing from the double-sided tape and stick the skyline to the front of the box, pressing it firmly in place **(drawing C)**. You now have a unique and whimsical piece of city art!

tips & hints

- *You can scale this to any size you'd like! Go big with an Empire State Building replica or stay homey.*

- *This is best displayed in the darker areas of your reception venue—think an empty corner or a subtly lighted hallway—to make the most of the LED lights.*

- *Search the Internet for free images of popular (and even obscure) skyline graphics. Google® Images and Flickr℠ are great resources.*

- *If the skyline is too big to print on your home computer, you can take it to Kinko's℠ or another copy center and have it printed for just a dollar or two.*

Price Breakdown

YOUR COST

Box	$4.00
Paint	$1.00
Paint brush	$1.00
LED lights	$6.00
Batteries	$3.00
Cardstock	$2.00
Transfer paper	$5.00
Tape	$3.00
TOTAL	**$25.00**

STORE COST

Custom card boxes cost upward of **$30.00** from specialty designers.

C.

Cardboard, 1" x 1" foam tape blocks affix to 4 corners of cutout back

Bottom of box

Cut a power source hole 1" x 2".

CHAPTER SEVEN: *Into the garden*

A GARDEN PARTY wedding needn't be all about high tea and crumpets. No, today's garden weddings are sweet, intimate affairs that pack quirky style into one fresh little package. In this chapter, you will learn how to create a lovely floral invitation using a block print technique to set the tone. Try a hand-painted monogram parasol to stylishly shield the sun from your and your bridesmaids' oh-so-delicate skin. Give a proposal of your own to your best girlfriends with the "Will You Be My Bridesmaid?" card, made with real flower petals. Combine old and new to create a stunning centerpiece from secondhand candlesticks and vintage teacups. Finally, send your wedding rings down the aisle in style with a garden-inspired no-sew ring pillow. Precious!

Together with their families

Xochitl Rodriguez

and

Abel Harmon

request the honor of your presence
at their marriage

on Saturday, the 20th of June

two thousand fifteen

at two o'clock in the afternoon

Berkeley Rose Gardens
Berkeley, California

Block Print Invitation

I've become something of a print nerd. Since taking a class on screen printing, I've been hooked on all forms of putting ink to paper. One of my new favorites, which is akin to the first wedding craft I ever did (rubber stamping), is linoleum block printing. It's marvelous as a gateway to other print techniques and a perfect way for beginner (and experienced) crafters to create killer invitations.

If you're a perfectionist who must have clean, perfect lines and precise placement or color, this may not be the technique for you. Linoleum, or block, printing is messy. It's often imperfect. It takes some time and trial and error to get right. But, for me and perhaps for you, this is part of what makes it so great.

With so much mechanized and homogenized perfection, it's so refreshing to give and receive items that look and feel handcrafted, like real, living human beings created them with their own hands. That's special and downright precious.

Block printing is exactly like it sounds: A block is used to put ink to paper. The block is a linoleum-faced piece of cork that's carved with a design. A rubber brayer is used to apply ink to the design, and then the block is put to paper. Ready to give it a go? Let's start!

CRAFTY COMMITMENT

3 hours for
25 invitations

SOLO A-GO-GO

Because you'll have extended drying times with the ink, allow yourself a full weekend or a few weeknight evenings to complete your invitations. Turn on the radio or invite your sweetie to read from your favorite book while you work.

SUPPLIES

- Computer with Microsoft Word
- Printer
- Watercolor paper, cut to 5 in. by 7 in.
- Pencil
- Linoleum block, 4 in. by 6 in., available from art stores
- Linoleum block cutter set
- Block printing ink
- Ink plate or a piece of glass
- Brayer
- Baren

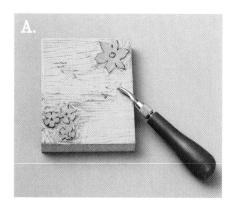

FIT YOUR STYLE

Having a country wedding? How about using a horseshoe motif for good luck?

DIRECTIONS

1. Start by printing a 5-in. by 7-in. invitation. Open Microsoft Word and create a new document. From the Page Setup menu, select "Custom Page Size" from the "Settings" options. Set the custom page size for "5" wide by "7" high. Click "OK."

2. Set the margin spacing to "0.50" for the left and right margins. For the top and bottom, set the margin spacing to "0.50." This will give you some blank space to apply your block print design. Click on the page and insert your invitation text. Save and print your invite on a 5-in. by 7-in. piece of watercolor paper.

3. Your next task is to come up with your design. You can create almost any style with linoleum printing, but bold designs with clear detail (nothing intricate) are the best bets, especially for beginners. Text is fine, as long as it's bold and you aren't looking for laser precision. It's important to note that your design will need to be in mirror image (backwards) of how you'll want it to print.

4. With a pencil, draw your design directly on the surface of the linoleum block. To help you determine where not to cut, color in the design with the pencil. With the linoleum cutters, remove all of the non-colored area around the design.

5. To cut away the linoleum, use firm, even strokes with the lino cutters. You needn't cut too deep. Let me warn you: This is hard work! Your hands and fingers will get fatigued. Take frequent breaks. And speaking of those fingers, lino cutters are wickedly sharp! Be extra-careful when you're cutting away the linoleum. Always carve away from you **(photo A)**.

6. When you're satisfied with your design, it's time to take it for a test print. Squeeze a small amount of ink onto the piece of glass or ink plate **(photo B)**. With your brayer, roll the ink out into a

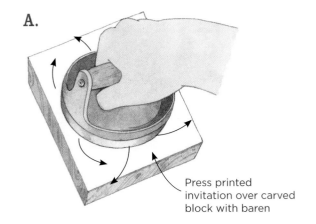

Press printed invitation over carved block with baren

smooth, thin layer. Carefully roll the inked brayer onto the surface of your block. All of the raised areas will accept the ink. Depending on how deeply you carved your design, you may end up with little carving lines showing in the background when you print. If it's not to your liking, go back and carve away those areas.

7. Place your printed invitation on top of the inked block. Using the baren, rub the paper with even pressure **(drawing A)**. This "pulls" the ink from the block onto the paper. Carefully peel the paper from the block and allow it to dry.

tips & hints

- *The best papers for linoleum prints are rag-based watercolor papers. They take ink very well and look beautiful.*

- *Linoleum inks come in limited colors, but they can be mixed to create custom shades.*

- *Have a backup block on hand in case you make a mistake*

(which is really easy to do, even for experienced printers).

- *Linoleum print ink is smelly. Work in a well-ventilated area whenever you can.*

- *The ink can get everywhere. Make sure you protect your work surface and clothing.*

Price Breakdown

YOUR COST

Watercolor paper	**$11.00**
Block	**$3.00**
Linoleum cutter set	**$12.00**
Ink	**$6.00**
Brayer	**$8.00**
Baren	**$5.00**

TOTAL	**$45.00**
	for 25 invitations or
	$1.80 each

STORE COST

Custom block print invitations can cost **$4.00** per invitation from custom stationers.

Paper Parasol

For most summertime brides, the small realities of having an outdoor ceremony and reception don't manifest until the very last weeks—or even days—before their weddings. In the months of May through August, I get a barrage of frantic emails from my readers that say something along the lines of:

"Uh oh! I'll be wearing a strapless gown at the beach on what's sure to be one of the hottest days of the year. How do I keep cool without sacrificing my status as a smokin' hot bride?"

One of the most-requested projects—and one I love to recommend for both brides and their guests—is the personalized paper parasol. A plain, rice paper parasol can be dolled up to create a customized accessory that not only protects your delicate skin from the harmful sun but also stands alone as a nifty prop for the abundant photo ops that are coming your way. Adding details like a quirky saying or even something like "thank you" is fun, and it looks cute.

CRAFTY COMMITMENT

3 hours plus drying time

SOLO A GO GO

Set aside a quiet evening to complete your parasol. Turn on your favorite music, pour yourself your favorite drink, and enjoy!

SUPPLIES

- Computer with Microsoft Word
- Printer
- Scissors
- Clear single-sided tape
- Transfer paper, available at art supply stores
- 28-in.-diameter paper parasol
- Painter's tape
- Soft lead pencil (#3 or higher)
- Paper plate
- Paint brushes
- Acrylic paint
- Gum eraser

DIRECTIONS

1. Start this project by creating the monogram you'd like to use in Microsoft Word. Open a new document and set it to landscape orientation in the Page Setup menu. Next, simply type in the letters or words you'd like to re-create on your parasol. If you're a font nerd like me, this is the fun part! You get to play around with fonts and styles. I like to work in a 72-point font to get an idea of how the letters will look when they're enlarged. You may work in any font size as long as it fits on the page. You'll be taking your printout to a copy shop in the next step to get it to the final size.

2. When you're satisfied with the font style, save the document and print it out. Take the printout to your local copy shop and have them enlarge it so that it fits within the 28-in. area you have to work with on the parasol. (The exact percentage will vary by your design and font selections.) Cut the design from the printed paper with scissors. This will serve as your template.

3. Once the template has been prepared, flip it over and tape the transfer paper to the back, making sure the transfer paper is facing upward so that when you flip it over, it makes contact with the parasol.

4. Open the parasol and lock it into the open position. Slip the template over the top knob and tape it down using painter's tape. Painter's tape (usually a bright blue) is low-tack tape, which means it has a temporary hold and can be removed easily **(drawing A)**.

FIT YOUR STYLE

Feeling more exotic? Try using a henna-inspired design to invoke the feeling of India and the Far East.

5. Using the soft lead pencil, trace over the template design onto the parasol. Don't press too hard or you'll poke through the parasol.

6. Now that you've created an outline of your design, you can begin the final step: painting. Place a generous dollop of paint onto a paper plate. Use thin layers of paint; too much will create soft spots in the delicate rice paper of the parasol, making it prone to tearing. I recommend dividing up the parasol into quarters and working on one section at a time, allowing each to dry before moving on to the next. It helps prevent smudging and, especially with an ornate design, gives your eyes and hands a break.

7. When the entire design is completely dry, use the gum eraser to gently erase any visible pencil lines from the parasol's surface.

A.

Cut center holes in template and transfer paper, then slip over parasol knob.

Template

28" area

Transfer paper

Use painter's tape to affix template to transfer paper and both to the parasol top.

tips & hints

- *Paper parasols come in all sorts of colors from white and natural to pastels and brights.*

- *Nearly any design can be used as long as you can fit it on the surface of the parasol. If ornate designs aren't your thing, how about "Love," "Just married," or "Thank you" as alternatives?*

- *If the thought of tracing a design bums you out, try a plastic stencil. They can be found in a tremendous array of styles and designs at craft stores and online stencil shops.*

- *Having a wedding in a humid climate? Consider using a spray fixative after your paint job has completely dried to help preserve your design. Water, unfortunately, is the sworn mortal enemy of paper parasols and acrylic paints.*

Price Breakdown

YOUR COST

Copy enlargement	**$1.00**
Transfer paper	**$6.00**
Paper parasol	**$8.00**
Acrylic paint	**$2.00**
TOTAL	**$17.00**

STORE COST

Custom-designed parasols start at **$35** from specialty designers.

"Will You Be My Bridesmaid?" Card

You've been through it all together, from bad break-ups (he broke up with her via Facebook℠) to the best triumphs (corner office with a salary to match) and everything in between. You've helped keep each other sane, you never have to worry about a ride to the airport, and you always, always have a trusted friend on your side.

When it comes time to ask your best gal pal to stand with you on your big day, it just makes sense to do it in a way that's totally you: with creativity and a bit of whimsy.

This "Will You Be My Bridesmaid?" card uses dried flower petals and parts to create an adorable representation of your bridesmaid-to-be on the cover; you pop the question to your girlfriend inside. It's flirty fun!

Drying flowers is fairly easy; all it takes is a microwave oven, some paper towels, and dinner plates. Not all flowers are suited for microwave drying, but lilies, roses, carnations, daisies, and hydrangea typically work well. Leaves work well, too, for those of you who want to take advantage of the bounty of richly colored foliage in the fall months. It may take some experimentation with different flowers and microwave times to get the right colors, shapes, and level of dryness, so be sure to buy or pick multiples of any flower you're thinking of using.

CRAFTY COMMITMENT
15 to 20 minutes
per card

SOLO A-GO-GO

This is a great project for a quiet morning at home. Grab a cup of coffee and spend some quality "me" time at the kitchen table.

SUPPLIES

- Pink cardstock, cut to 4¼ in. by 11 in.
- Bone folder
- Ink pen
- Flowers and leaves of your choice
- Microwave
- Paper towels
- Microwave-safe plate
- Perfect Paper Adhesive™ glue
- Thin, soft paint brush
- Tweezers
- White watercolor paper, cut to 3¾ in. by 5 in.
- Red cardstock, cut to 4 in. by 5¼ in.
- Double-sided tape

A.

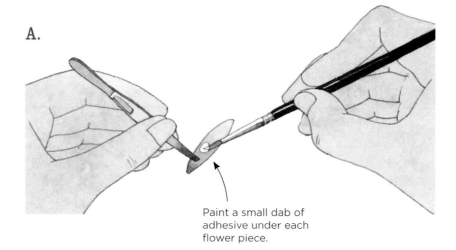

Paint a small dab of adhesive under each flower piece.

DIRECTIONS

1. Kick off this project by getting your card bases ready. Fold the 4¼-in. by 11-in. pink cardstock in half and crease with a bone folder. Now is a good time to write your sentiments on the inside in case you make a mistake. It's better to err at this point than to mess up a card that has a completed floral design.

2. The next step is the flower-drying process. Because each microwave is different and each flower has different water content, fiber structure, and density, this is a trial-and-error process. To dry flowers, place a double layer of paper towels on a microwave-safe dish. Gently place your blooms on top of the paper towel layers, and then place another double layer of paper towels on top of them. Place the plate in the microwave and microwave for 40 seconds on high power (20 seconds for very delicate flowers). Check to see if the flowers feel dry (but not crisp). If they still feel damp, put them back in for another 10 seconds. Let the flowers cool before you start using them.

3. Once your flowers are dry and cool, you can start creating your floral masterpiece. See the photo on page 174 for a sample layout. On the front of one of the folded cards, gently arrange your floral material to create a pretty little figure. Don't be afraid to move pieces around to see what works best for your design.

4. Using Perfect Paper Adhesive and the paint brush, gently lift up the pieces with tweezers and paint a small dab of adhesive under each piece to secure it to the watercolor paper **(drawing A)**. Gently press each piece into place. Set the card aside to dry completely.

5. When the petals are completely dry, it's time to complete the card assembly. Adhere the watercolor and petal paper to the red cardstock, centering it top to bottom and left to right with double-sided tape. Now adhere this stack to the front of your folded cardstock. Well done!

tips & hints

- *Don't get discouraged if you scorch a bloom or an ultra-pretty petunia turns a grimy brown. Try again! Make small adjustments to the microwave time or use different flowers.*

- *Not all flowers are microwave-friendly. Roses, lilies, pansies, daisies, hydrangea, and bougainvillea tend to work well. Ferns and leaves are also great for drying and add lovely color and texture to a design.*

- *Flowers will change color as they dry. They tend to become darker and "muddier."*

- *Flowers that are fresh and unblemished work best. Any discolorations and imperfections will look magnified after the drying process.*

Price Breakdown

YOUR COST

Pink and red cardstock	**$3.00**
1 bunch mixed flowers	**$7.00**
1 pad of watercolor paper	**$4.00**
1 bottle of Perfect Paper Adhesive	**$7.00**
Double-sided tape	**$4.00**

TOTAL   **$25.00**
for about 5 cards or about **$5.00** each

STORE COST
Generic bridesmaid cards cost about **$3.00** each at stationery shops.

Teacup Centerpiece

"**H**i, Khris!" Meghan wrote. "I scored 65 teacups from my grandmother's church's tag sale. My 100-guest garden wedding is in April. How do I incorporate these into my decor in a way that will allow me to use them later?"

Meg had originally planned on using groups of small potted plants and candles as her centerpieces. My solution was to place the teacups and saucers on top of painted candlesticks, using those as the containers for the plants and candles in her centerpiece. She loved it!

Re-creating this project for the book, however, was a big challenge. Vintage teacups can be quite expensive. I highly recommend that you start collecting months in advance to give yourself time to find the right (that is, pretty) teacups that won't cost an arm and a leg. Seriously, some teacups in less than mint condition go for more than $20 each! Most of the ones I found were in the $4.00 to $10.00 range at flea markets.

The beauty of this project is that it's a beginner-level craft. Anyone can do it and make it look fabulous. For this project, you'll need to puddle the glue around the rim of the candlestick and on the bottom of the china to make a solid seal that will last through the big day.

CRAFTY COMMITMENT

2 to 3 hours

CRAFTY COUPLE

Even the least crafty guy can get on board with this project. Grab your guy and set him to the task of spraying and gluing while you add the finishing touches. Or vice versa!

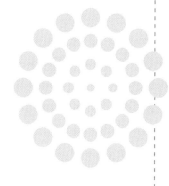

SUPPLIES

- 5 teacups and saucers
- 5 candlesticks, varied heights
- Newspaper
- 1 can spray primer, white
- 1 can spray paint, white
- Hot glue gun and hot glue
- Plants and candles as filler for the teacups

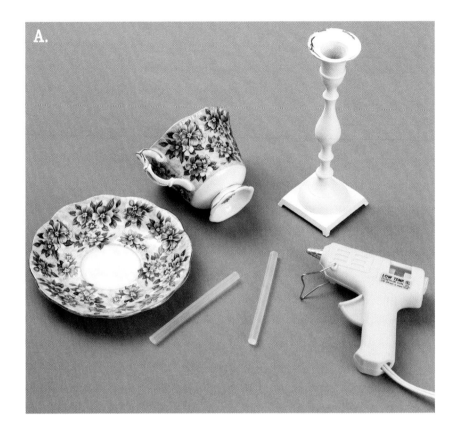

A.

DIRECTIONS

1. Clean the cups, saucers, and candlesticks in warm, soapy water. Rinse and dry.

2. In a well-ventilated area, place the candlesticks on a layer of newspaper to protect your work surface. Spray the candlesticks with a coat of primer per the manufacturer's directions. Allow to dry. Follow with 2 to 3 coats of spray paint, allowing each coat to fully dry before moving on to the next.

3. Using the hot glue gun, place a ring of hot glue on the top rim of the candlestick and the bottom rim of the teacup **(photo A)**.

4. Place the saucer on top of the candlestick and the teacup on top of the saucer. Press them together firmly, then allow them to cool. Repeat for the remaining candlesticks and china pieces. Easy-peasy, right?

5. To display, put a group of 5 candlesticks in the center of the table. Place a plant, cut flowers, or a candle in the cups.

tips & hints

- The best (and cheapest) spots to find teacups: garage sales, a grandma's attic, flea markets, tag sales, Craigslist^{SM}. Antique stores and eBay usually offer the best selection, but their wares are often higher-end collectibles that are expensive.

- Secondhand stores are great places to pick up used candlesticks in every shape, style, and size imaginable. The most I paid for a candlestick was $2.00. One store owner even gave me a matching set for free just to get rid of them. Candlesticks get no secondhand love!

- When you're ready to remove the teacups from the candlesticks, soak them in warm water for a few hours. The teacups should separate from the candlesticks with little resistance. If they're stubborn, leave them overnight. Still not budging? That's a risk. You can try a commercial solvent like Goo Gone® or acetone polish remover as a last resort.

Price Breakdown

YOUR COST

Teacups and saucers	**$20.00**
Candlesticks	**$5.00**
Primer	**$4.00**
Paint	**$4.00**
Hot glue	**$4.00**
Plants and accessories	**$10.00**

TOTAL	**$47.00**
for a set of 5 candlesticks	

STORE COST

I have not yet seen anything like these on the market. However, a custom floral centerpiece can cost upward of **$80.00** from a florist.

FIT YOUR STYLE

Try jelly jars instead of teacups for a country wedding.

No-Sew Ring Pillow

If the mere thought of using a sewing machine makes you break out in hives or if a needle and thread is your sworn mortal enemy, I've got a fab little no-sew project that makes it look like you've got mad skills in the needle arts.

Like most couples, you're on board with sending your precious ring bearer down the aisle with a ring pillow. Not just any pillow will do, though. You want something custom-tailored to your wedding, and there are just not a lot of options on the market that suit your particular tastes.

This sweet little pillow may just be what you're looking for! It's made from sheets of felt, a little pillow stuffing called fiber fill, and a glue gun, so you can be well on your way to becoming a ring pillow designer without getting anywhere near a needle and thread.

The pillow can be completed in a few hours and requires no previous craft experience. If you can use a ruler and scissors, you can make this pillow!

CRAFTY COMMITMENT

2 to 3 hours

SOLO A-GO-GO

Throw on your sweats and sit in front of the TV for an afternoon for this project. Don't get too involved in your DVR soaps, though; you've got hot glue to watch out for!

SUPPLIES

- Hot glue gun and hot glue
- 2 sheets of wool felt in white, 9 in. by 12 in.
- Ruler
- Fabric marker
- Pinking shears
- Fiber fill stuffing
- 1 or 2 sheets of 8½-in. by 11-in. paper or cardstock, for templates
- Scissors
- 5 sheets of wool felt, each in a different color, for blooms and leaves, 9 in. by 12 in.
- ⅝-in.-wide ribbon, 12 in. long

DIRECTIONS

1. Start heating your glue gun while you begin the first step of this project. Place 2 pieces of white felt together and set them on a flat surface. Using a ruler and fabric marker, draw an 8-in. square in the middle of the felt. Cut out the square on both pieces of felt with pinking shears. Cutting both layers together ensures that both sides have the "tooth" pattern from the pinking shears evenly aligned.

2. On one of the squares you've just cut, mark lines ½ in. from the edges along each side using the ruler and fabric marker. These will serve as your glue guidelines and will be on the inside of your ring pillow (**drawing A**).

3. Using the glue gun, run a long, thin line of hot glue along one of the guidelines you just drew to the point where the lines connect on each side. You don't want to glue all the way from edge to edge (**drawing A**). Working quickly, before the glue cools, align the edges of your top sheet of felt over the bottom sheet and press the sheets together over the glue line. Repeat on two more sides, leaving one side open for the moment.

4. Once your three sides are glued into place and dry, insert a small handful or two of fiber fill stuffing into the cavity of the pillow. Less is more here; you don't want a big, puffy pillow, just a slightly plump one.

5. When you're satisfied with the pillow plumpness, add the fourth line of glue and seal the pillow. Pretty easy, right?

6. Here's where the fun begins: decorating! I've provided 4 different bloom (**drawings D, E, F and G**) and 2 leaf templates (**drawings B and C**) for you to create fabulous felt flowers to embellish your pillow. These, like the pillow, are done with a glue gun.

A.

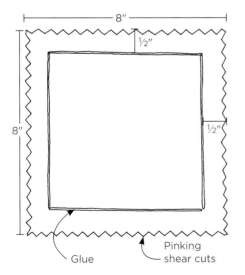

B.

C.

D.

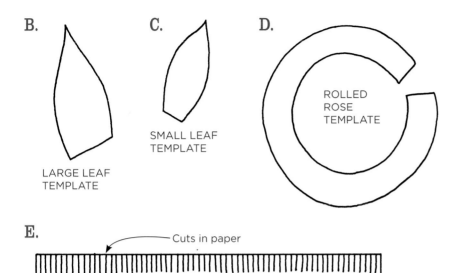

LARGE LEAF
TEMPLATE

SMALL LEAF
TEMPLATE

ROLLED
ROSE
TEMPLATE

F.

FUSCHIA AND LILY TEMPLATE

Petals for
fuschia

Enlarge
50 percent
for lily

E.

Cuts in paper

ROLLED FLOWER TEMPLATE

G.

PINK FLOWER TEMPLATE

Cut in center

For the rolled rose and rolled flower (drawings D and E):

Copy the templates onto paper or cardstock and cut them out.

Trace the templates onto your chosen color of felt and snip
them out with scissors.

Using hot glue, apply a small dollop on the end of one side
and roll the felt into a concentric circle, applying another dab of
glue on the other end to affix it to itself **(drawing H)**.

For the fuchsia (drawing F):

Cut 6 circles out of felt using my templates as your guide.

continued on p. 186

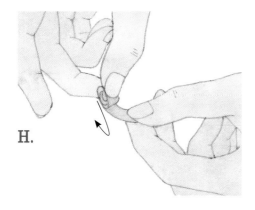

H.

Near the bottom edge of each circle, working one at a time, place a tiny bit of hot glue and pinch the sides of the circle together to make a petal.

After all of your petals are created, it's time to glue them together to form a flower. Add a small amount of glue on each side of the petal, near the centermost point, and stick it to the next petal until you have a full circle **(drawing I)**.

For the lily (drawing F):

Cut 1 circle from the large template.

I.

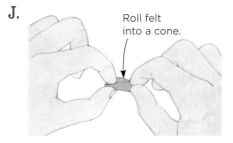

Hot glue in center

Glue gun

Near the bottom edge of the circle, place a tiny bit of hot glue and roll the felt like a cone to make the lily bloom **(drawing J)**.

For the pink flower (drawing G):

Cut a flower from the template.

Along the cut line, as shown on the template, snip it with your scissors.

Add a small drop of hot glue near one of the snipped edges and fold the flower up and slightly roll it onto itself. This makes the flower 3-dimensional **(drawing K)**.

J.

Roll felt into a cone.

7. Now place a large drop of glue on the bottom of each flower and leaf and press it onto the top of the pillow. Hold it in place (usually just a few seconds) until it has cooled and is securely affixed.

8. The final touch is to affix a 12-in. length of ribbon so that you have a place to tie the rings to. Fold the ribbon in half, apply a drop of hot glue, and stick it onto the center of the pillow **(photo A)**.

tips & hints

- *This project works well with heavier-weight fabrics. Think wool, heavy cotton, fleece, suiting, and upholstery fabrics because they don't show the glue lines as much as more delicate fabrics will.*

- *If you're not into flowery things, explore a die-cutting machine and dies to add unique designs (without all that pesky cutting) that may better suit your theme.*

- *I prefer wool felts over synthetic felts because they look and feel more luxe, and synthetics have a tendency to melt under the heat of the hot glue.*

- *Select a "disappearing" fabric marker. These are found at craft stores or in fabric stores. Be careful, though: The ink shows up for only 24 hours, so get the cutting done that day.*

K.

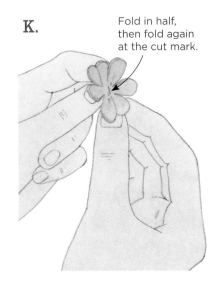

Fold in half, then fold again at the cut mark.

A.

Price Breakdown

YOUR COST

Hot glue	**$1.00**
7 pieces of felt ($3.00 each)	**$21.00**
Fabric marker	**$2.00**
Fiber fill	**$5.00**
1 spool of ribbon	**$3.00**
TOTAL	**$32.00**

STORE COST

Custom felt ring pillows cost **$40.00** from bridal accessory designers.

FIT YOUR STYLE

Winter wedding couples can use darker, richer colors for a cozier feel. How about a dark gray pillow with red, orange, indigo, and dark green flowers and foliage?

CHAPTER EIGHT: *The New Modern*

WHILE SIMPLE LINES and minimalism typically define a modern look, I wanted to put a DIY Bride spin on it here to make it more accessible and inviting. Modern isn't stark or cold; it's warm and welcoming. Today's modern weddings combine sleek, sophisticated elements with unusual textures, materials, and even a sense of the past to create something fresh and unique while remaining visually uncluttered. Start off married life with a silver ring that's handmade from a special clay and is beautifully textured with sandpaper. Create a stunning backdrop to your cocktail lounge or cake table with a curtain made of luxurious double-satin ribbon in hot mod colors. Adorn the men in the bridal party with boutonnieres made with the unusual coneflower and dyed foliage. Mix the old and exotic, faux mercury glass and tropical protea blooms, to create a decidedly modern centerpiece. End your perfect day by bidding your guests a fond farewell with a modern take on the traditional piece of cake: a wedding cake-pop favor. Every ending should be so sweet!

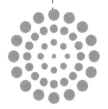

Modern Wedding Cake Pops

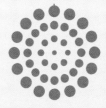

When an elaborate wedding cake is just too much and when cupcakes just seem way overdone, what's a sophisticated, clever modern couple to serve to their discerning guests? Cake pops!

I discovered these gems when searching for ideas for my toddler's birthday party. What's a cake pop? They're yummy bits of cakey goodness on a stick, that's what they are! Bits of cake and icing are mixed together to make a sort of truffle, and then they are dipped in a coating and presented like a lollipop. While the *Sesame Street*–inspired treats I found for my son's birthday aren't exactly appropriate for most modern weddings, when stripped of their Muppet-ness, cake pops can be a terrific (and stylish) alternative to more traditional cake options. They're fab as favors, too.

CRAFTY COMMITMENT

2 to 3 hours
per 50 cake truffles

WITH A LITTLE HELP FROM MY FRIENDS

This is a great assembly-line project. Gather together a small army of helpers to form, dip, and decorate your yummy treats.

SUPPLIES

- 1 box vanilla cake mix
- 4 egg whites
- 1 cup sugar
- Stand mixer or electric hand mixer
- 3 sticks unsalted butter, at room temperature
- 1 tsp. vanilla extract
- Mini ice cream scooper or tablespoon
- 1 or 2 packages each of white and orange candy melts
- Fifty 4-in. lollipop sticks
- 1 large piece of craft foam, for holding the pops-in-progress
- Food coloring (optional)
- Sprinkles (optional)
- 1 clear acrylic photo frame box, 11 in. by 14 in.
- 1 piece of 1-in.-thick craft foam, cut to 10 in. by 13 in.
- One 5-lb. box of rock salt

DIRECTIONS

1. Bake the cake according to the package directions and let it cool completely before you begin making the pops. Enjoy the scent of warm, delicious cake in your kitchen.

2. While the cake is cooling, get started on the frosting. Set a small glass or metal bowl over a pan of gently boiling water 1 to 2 in. deep. With a whisk, combine the egg whites and the sugar in the bowl, stirring constantly until the sugar has dissolved, about 3 minutes. The mixture should resemble marshmallow cream.

3. Pour the mixture into the bowl of a stand mixer fitted with the whisk attachment. If you're sans stand mixer (put one on your registries right now, friends; they're the cat's meow of kitchen gadgets), go ahead and use an electric hand mixer. Whip on medium speed until the mixture has cooled and forms a thick, shiny meringue, about 5 minutes.

4. Stop the mixer and swap the whisk attachment for a paddle attachment. On medium speed, add the butter, 1 tablespoon at a time, mixing until completely incorporated after each addition. Add the vanilla and mix on medium-high speed for about 5 minutes, until the frosting is light and completely smooth.

5. Now we can start making pops! When the cake is at room temperature, crumble it into a large bowl until it's broken up into small, pea-size pieces. Using your fingers or a wooden spoon, mix in 1¼ cups of the frosting to start with. Mix until the frosting is evenly dispersed throughout the cake. The texture should be very moist and sticky.

6. Using a tablespoon or a mini ice cream scooper, scoop out a ball of the cake mixture. Roll it between your palms into a ball. If it stays together, continue to roll the rest of your cake mixture into balls and place them on a parchment- or wax paper–lined baking

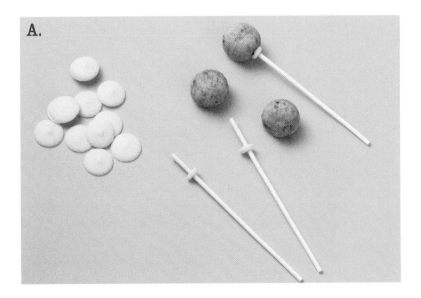

A.

sheet. If they fall apart or do not hold together, add a little more frosting until the mix is moist enough to allow you to roll an intact ball.

7. Once you have rolled all of the cake mix into balls, place them in the refrigerator and chill for 30 to 60 minutes. When the cake balls have chilled, melt a small amount of the candy melts in a microwave-safe bowl according to the package directions.

8. Take one of the sticks, dip ¼ in. to ½ in. of the end into the melted candy, then stick it about halfway through the cake pop **(photo A)**.

9. Place the cake pop into a piece of foam, stick side down, so that the pop part is facing upward and can harden.

10. Now the cake balls go into the freezer for 15 to 30 minutes before getting their candy coating. Freezing the balls will keep them intact while they're being dipped in the hot candy melts.

continued on p. 194

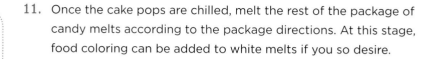

11. Once the cake pops are chilled, melt the rest of the package of candy melts according to the package directions. At this stage, food coloring can be added to white melts if you so desire.

12. Dip the cake pops, one at a time, into the melted candy coating. I like to roll them in it to help ensure the entire ball gets coated. Do make sure to get the coating all the way to where the stick meets the ball so that they're firmly stuck together. You don't want rogue cake balls escaping from the display later on.

13. To get an even layer all the way around, rotate the cake pop while gently tapping off any excess coating on the edge of the bowl. If you're adding sprinkles, now is the time to do so, while the coating is still warm and sticky. Either shake the sprinkles over the cake truffles or gently dip each cake ball into a container of sprinkles. Shaking will give you less sprinkles; dipping will give more coverage.

14. Set the pops back in the foam and put them in the refrigerator to harden. Keep cool until serving time.

15. For the display, we're using a clear acrylic photo frame as a tray. These are available at craft and discount stores. They're like a box without a back. When turned over on their backs, they make a great (and cheap) serving tray. Cut a piece of 1-in.-thick foam that's 1 in. shorter than the inner dimensions of your tray. For an 11-in. by 14-in. tray, the foam should be cut to 10 in. by 13 in.

16. Set the foam inside of the tray cavity, centering it on all sides. Between the sides and the foam, add rock salt until it's even with the foam and top of the tray. Insert your cake truffles into the foam. Add a layer of salt over the top of the foam to cover it. Your cake masterpieces are ready to display!

tips & hints

- I've used a box cake for convenience in the instructions, but homemade cakes work wonderfully for this project as well. I prefer from-scratch cakes for flavor, texture, and ingredient control. If you love boxed cake mixes, then absolutely use those!

- Angel food cake is really the only cake I've found that doesn't work well, because it's too light in combination with the frosting.

- One of the great things about cake pops is that you can make them out of any cake and frosting flavor combination. Some of my favorites are green tea cake with ginger frosting, peanut butter cake with banana frosting, honey-almond cake with strawberry frosting, and caramel cake with macchiato frosting.

- Candy melts are basically flavored and colored cocoa butter that's been made shelf-stable. You can substitute chocolate (dark, milk, or white) for the candy melts. I do recommend adding a bit of cocoa butter to the chocolate as both an extender and to make it smoother for dipping.

- Foam sheets can be found at all major craft stores.

- If clear trays aren't to your liking, you can use nearly any kind of container to display your treats: galvanized trays, buckets, baskets, vintage dishes, cigar boxes, fabric- or paper-covered cardboard boxes, and so on.

- Don't limit yourself to sprinkles for decoration! Dragées, seeds, sanding sugar, crushed candies, chopped nuts, edible flower petals, and icing can all be used.

- Though I've heard reports of these staying fresh for weeks, I highly recommend making these no more than 3 days in advance of your serving date. Keep them refrigerated at all times until display!

Price Breakdown

YOUR COST

Cake	$3.00
Frosting ingredients	$2.00
Candy melts	$5.00
Sticks	$4.00
Foam	$6.00
Sprinkles	$6.00
Frame	$8.00
Rock salt	$1.00
TOTAL	**$35.00**
	for 60 pops or
	$0.58 each

STORE COST

Cake pops cost anywhere from **$1.50** to **$3.00** per pop from cake designers.

Precious Metal Clay Ring

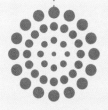

You, my modern couple, are eco-friendly and design-conscious. Your wedding is all about personality, sustainability, and style. That's why not just any wedding ring will do. After scouring the markets for jewelry companies with eco-friendly practices that have rings that don't scream generic, you're not left with many affordable options. So why not try your hand at creating your own ring?

Relatively new to the crafting market is something called metal clay. It's most often finely ground silver that's mixed with an organic binder that burns off when it's fired to leave 99 percent pure silver behind. You can use it to create a vast array of jewelry and decorative items—including a very special and very personal ring for your beloved.

Though it may sound a bit intimidating, you already have most of the skills for this project. If you played with Play-Doh® as a kid, you're halfway there. If you can roll out pie dough, even better. Can you use a paint brush? Awesome. Can you point a flame at something and use a timer? Perfect! You're qualified to become your own personal jeweler!

CRAFTY COMMITMENT

8 to 24 hours

SOLO A-GO-GO

Set aside some uninterrupted time to play with your metal clay. Be careful! Precious metal clay can be so fun to work with that it's addictive. Do account for drying time when planning for your foray into jewelry making.

SUPPLIES

- Copier
- Deck of playing cards
- Clear single-sided tape
- Wood ring mandrel
- Wax paper
- Nonstick mat
- Olive oil
- Precious metal clay PMC3, 9g package
- Acrylic rolling pin, found in the clay section at craft stores
- Tissue blade or X-ACTO craft knife
- Zip-top bag or airtight container
- A sheet of sandpaper
- Small paint brush
- Electronic mug warmer
- Small metal file set, found in the jewelry section at craft stores
- Small bowl of cool water
- Solderite™ firing board, found at PMC clay retailers
- Small butane torch and fuel
- Stopwatch or digital timer
- Pliers or long-handled tweezers
- Steel wire brush, found in hardware stores

DIRECTIONS

1. The first step is to determine the size of your ring. With a strip of paper that's cut to ¼ in. wide, wrap it around your beloved's finger, making sure it fits over his knuckle. With an ink pen, mark where the end meets the complete circumference of his finger.

2. Enlarge the piece of paper on a copier by 10 percent. PMC3 will shrink during the firing process, so you need to add extra length to account for the shrinkage. Once your paper has been copied, cut your ring template out. At this point, you can trim the ring width (not length!) to your preferred size on the template. Make sure your cut is even.

3. This step may seem a bit odd, but don't worry! It's an important one that will help make your project a success. Put together 2 stacks of playing cards, each with 6 cards. Tape each stack together. These will serve as a guide to ensure your clay has an even thickness throughout.

4. Get your mandrel prepped by wrapping a single layer of wax paper around it and taping it in place. This will help prevent the ring from sticking to it while it's drying.

5. Now you can get started with creating the ring. Moisten your hands, the nonstick mat work surface, and the rolling and cutting tools with a tiny bit of olive oil. This serves two purposes: It helps prevent the clay from sticking to everything and it helps prevent

FIT YOUR STYLE

Use a faux bois rubber stamp to create a wood-grain look for a garden or other outdoorsy themed wedding.

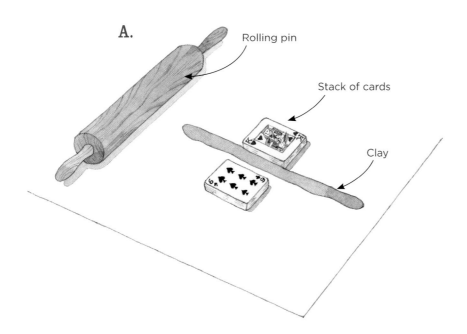

A.

Rolling pin

Stack of cards

Clay

it from drying out too quickly. If you use too much oil, a quick dab with a paper towel should wick up the excess. The bonus with all of this? Olive oil is great for those of us with dry hands. Your skin will thank you.

6. Using your hands, roll the lump of clay until it is long and skinny, like the snakes you made with Play-Doh when you were a kid.

7. Place your skinny clay snake between the 2 layers of cards **(drawing A)**. Use the acrylic rolling pin to flatten the clay to the height of the cards by pressing firmly down and rolling straight out. Don't sweat it if the clay extends past the top of the card: That's fine; you can trim it later. If the clay gets a little dry, dab a drop of water on its surface. Be careful here, as the clay becomes very sticky when it gets wet. Let the water absorb for a minute before playing with it again.

continued on p. 200

8. Once the clay is rolled out and is smooth, place the paper ring template on top of it. Using the tissue blade, cut away all of the excess clay around the template. Immediately put all of the scrap clay in the zip-top bag. You can save it and use it for other projects.

9. Don't move the clay for the ring just yet. It's time to add the texture that makes this project so cool. Gently lay the piece of sandpaper on top of the clay. Using the rolling pin and the card stacks as thickness guides again, press the sandpaper onto the surface of the clay. Gently remove the sandpaper.

10. Now, for the hardest part, gently remove the clay from your work surface and wrap it around the mandrel until the strip just barely overlaps **(drawing B)**. Using the tissue blade, cut through the overlapped clay at an angle.

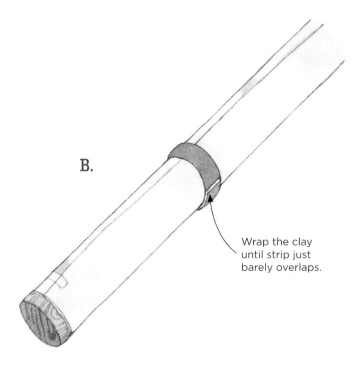

B.

Wrap the clay until strip just barely overlaps.

11. Moisten the cut edges with a tiny bit of water and press them together to join. If the seam is not perfect, don't worry about it yet. You can fill in cracks or smooth imperfections as the ring dries.

12. After the ring is formed on the mandrel, let it dry until it holds its shape. This can take anywhere from 20 minutes to more than an hour. The clay will start to turn lighter in color as it dries. A uniformly light color is a good indicator that it is in the "holding its shape" stage. This is the time to fill in cracks and reinforce the seam if necessary. To do so, using the paint brush, mix a tiny bit of water with a tiny chunk of clay to make a paste. This paste is called *slip*, and it is used to fill in the gaps and imperfections. Let the ring dry until it returns to the "holding its shape" stage again, then gently remove it from the mandrel.

13. Plug in your mug warmer and turn it on. Place the ring directly on the warmer's surface. This handy gadget will dry the clay ring completely and quickly to prepare it for the firing step. The ring should achieve what's known as the "leather-hard" stage, when there's no visible moisture and the PMC feels solid without any bending or movement with gentle handling, in 15 to 20 minutes, though it may take longer.

14. When the ring is leather-hard, remove it from the mug warmer and turn the warmer off. Let the ring cool for a couple of minutes. You may now gently sand and file the edges and interior of the ring to remove any sharp parts or imperfections. I know I keep repeating "gently" in these steps, but it's important to remember that until the clay is fired it is quite fragile and can break or crumble. You've made it this far! Pat yourself on the back and get prepped for the next step, which is a fun one: playing with fire!

15. Since this step involves an open flame, you may want to do this outside or on a surface that's not a prized family heirloom. Do

continued on p. 202

Price Breakdown

YOUR COST

Mandrel	$9.00
PMC3	$20.00
Acrylic rolling pin	$5.00
Tissue blade	$8.00
Mug warmer	$5.00
File set	$6.00
Firing board	$9.25
Butane torch	$15.00
Steel wire brush	$3.00
TOTAL	**$80.25**

STORE COST
Custom silver rings can cost anywhere from **$40** to **$400**, depending on the retailer.

make sure you have proper ventilation in the room, as the firing process will yield a bit of smoke. Have a container of water on hand to dunk the hot ring into when the firing is done. Set the firing board on a flat, even surface. Place the ring in the center of the board. Turn on your torch.

16. Ready to get all pyro on this thing? Holding the torch a few inches away from the ring, aim the flame directly on top of the ring, constantly but slowly moving it around the entire surface of the ring. Your goal is to give the ring even, consistent heat. The flame should be touching the ring while you're doing this, and you'll need to constantly monitor how close the flame is and how hot the ring is getting. Try to stay just in the red flame area; the blue part of the flame is generally too hot and will melt the ring.

17. After a couple of minutes, your piece will start burning and go up in flames. This happens very quickly. *Do not freak!* It's supposed to do this. The organic binders in the clay are burning off, leaving pure silver behind. Cool, right?

18. Keep torching the ring. It will start glowing a melon-ish, reddish color. Start your timer and keep firing for another 3 minutes or according to the manufacturer's recommended firing time. The piece should be glowing evenly, without any visible cool spots or areas that look as though they're melting. Remember to keep the whole ring evenly heated by moving your torch around.

19. Your ring has now been fired. It's a genuine metal ring now! *DO NOT* touch it or pick it up with your fingers. It is dangerously hot. Use tweezers or pliers to grab it and plunge it in cool water. Leave it for a few minutes and then pull it out. It will appear to be white. That's just a layer of smoke and binder.

20. Using the steel wire brush, scrub away the white layer of gunk from the ring. The silver will appear as the layer is brushed away.

tips & hints

- There are different brands and types of metal clay, and each one is very different from the others in terms of shrinkage and firing. The directions for this project are written specifically for PMC3 and may not work with any other brand or PMC type.

- If silver isn't your thing, metal clays now come in gold, copper, and bronze. Be sure to read the package directions for firing and shrinkage. Not all metal clays are suitable for torch firing; some may need to be fired in a kiln.

- As PMC contains silver, its cost rises and falls with the international silver market. PMC pricing can change from day to day on your favorite PMC sites. There's nothing you or the retailers can do about it, but it's something you should be aware of.

- If you goof, you can start all over with PMC at any point before you fire it with a torch. It's pretty forgiving that way.

- The question I get about this project time and time again is about the torch. You don't need anything sophisticated; a crème brûlée torch from your local hardware conglomerate or housewares store is just fine. The cheap ones work just as well as the expensive ones. Buy one that feels right in your hands. Bonus: You can make crème brûlée on a whim now.

- Nearly anything can be used to make an impression in metal clay. Leaves, rubber stamps, fabric, buttons, needles for writing text, impression mats, tree bark—don't be afraid to experiment!

- Keep your clay in a cool, damp, airtight container. Because it's so expensive, you'll want to save every scrap, every bit of filing and flakes; they can be reused over and over until they're fired.

- To rehydrate dried-out clay, wrap it in a slightly damp paper towel and put it in a zip-top bag overnight. The clay will become moist and pliable again.

- Rings aren't the only items you can make from metal clay. Charms, bracelets, earrings, and necklaces are among the awesome items you can craft now that you've got the skills.

- The firing block is specially designed to absorb all of the heat during the torch firing. It's safe to place on household surfaces while you work. If you're uneasy about doing so, work outside with the saucer of a clay pot underneath the firing block for extra protection.

- Do work in a well-ventilated space when firing. The puff of smoke may set off fire alarms if you're too close. I work in my kitchen with the stove's exhaust fan going, which works out just fine.

- Don't expect perfection the first time around. Sometimes working with a new medium takes some time to get right. Give yourself permission (and time!) to play around with the clay before you commit to firing to get a feel for it.

Ribbon Wall Curtain

While scouting online for wedding locations, we found a near-perfect venue overlooking the San Francisco Bay. Seeing the venue in person, however, proved to be a much different experience. The rooms seemed impossibly smaller. The parking lot had only about half the spots we'd need. The real deal breaker was the glorious reception room. Yes, it had that million-dollar view, but what wasn't shown in the photos was the pink-hued flocked wallpaper reminiscent of Pepto-Bismol®. I swear on all things design and holy that this is true.

Through the years I've learned that few venues are picture-perfect. Oftentimes it takes the efforts of event designers and florists to transform a ho-hum venue into the ultra-stylish rooms you see in bridal magazines and sales brochures. While that's fine and dandy if you've got a big budget, those of us watching our pennies need quick and inexpensive ideas to perk up a plain white wall or to soften industrial features in an otherwise stylish location.

My go-to project is a curtain made of wood dowels and ribbon. Hung with removable peel-and-stick hooks, this is an easy way to create a stylish backdrop at nearly any event. This project creates a 6-ft.-wide by 7-ft.-tall curtain.

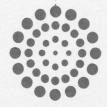

CRAFTY COMMITMENT

3 hours

CRAFTY COUPLE

An extra pair of hands is essential for measuring out the ribbon. Grab your guy or gal and schedule some "us" time to make this ultra-cool backdrop for your one-of-a-kind wedding.

SUPPLIES

- Hot glue gun and glue
- 1½-in. unwired red, gray, and white double-satin ribbon, 50-yd. spools of each
- Scissors
- Tape measure
- Two 36-in. dowels, ¾ in. in diameter
- Liquid fray preventer (optional)
- 4 large Command™ removable peel-and-stick hooks

FIT YOUR STYLE

Beach-wedding couples can use ribbons in watery shades of blue. A tropical wedding? Mix bold fuchsias, purples, citrus greens, and oranges.

DIRECTIONS

1. Plug in your glue gun and let it heat up while you're working on the ribbon.

2. To get started, you'll need to know the dimensions of the area you want to cover. The length of ribbon and the width of the rods will depend on your space. I recommend working in sections that are 7 ft. to 8 ft. tall by 6 ft. wide.

3. The toughest part of this project is where you begin, by cutting the ribbon to length. It's best to grab a partner for this part of the project. An extra pair of hands will help hold the ribbon and tape measure in place while the other partner does the unrolling and cutting of the ribbon. Roll out a 7-ft. (or however long you've decided) length of ribbon and cut it with a sharp pair of scissors.

4. Lay one of the dowels on the floor and arrange the ribbon as you'd like it to hang, untangling the ribbon as you go so that it lies flat.

5. Once you're satisfied with the ribbon order, it's time to put that glue gun to use! One by one, glue the strips of ribbon to the dowel, being careful to place the dollops of hot glue in roughly the same place along the length of the dowel **(drawing A)**. This will help all of the ribbon strips remain at the same length when you're done.

6. Now that all of the ribbon has been adhered to the dowel, repeat on the second dowel. You'll end up with 6 ft. by 7 ft. of curtain.

7. You'll notice that the top of the curtain, along the dowel, may look a bit rough and unfinished. Cut a 36-in. strip of ribbon and glue it horizontally along the top of the dowel to cover the unfinished edges **(drawing B)**. If you find the bottom edges of the ribbon are

A.

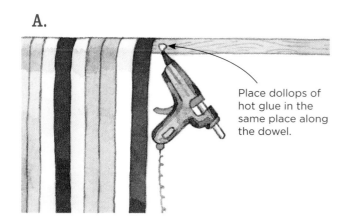

Place dollops of hot glue in the same place along the dowel.

B.

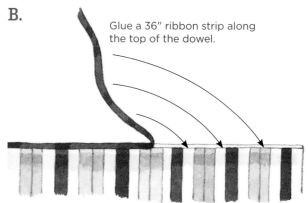

Glue a 36″ ribbon strip along the top of the dowel.

fraying, apply a liquid anti-fray product (available from craft and fabric stores) to keep them nice and tidy.

8. To hang the ribbon curtain, remove the protective backs from the Command hooks, then stick them to a wall. Have a friend or two on hand to help hang the hooks and the curtains.

tips & hints

- *Double-satin ribbon comes in numerous widths and colors. Go all-out with unique combinations of colors and sizes!*

- *I prefer double-satin ribbon over single-satin because it has more heft and hangs better. It's generally prettier, too.*

- *Single-satin ribbon is often less expensive and can be used for this project. You may need to attach small weights (available at sports shops in the fishing section) to the bottom of each ribbon strip to help hold it in place when the curtain is hung. This is also a good tip for those of you using the ribbon curtains outside, to help keep the breeze from wreaking havoc.*

- *The removable hooks are friendly to most surfaces. However, check with your ceremony or reception venue to make sure you're allowed to attach the curtains this way.*

Price Breakdown

YOUR COST

Hot glue	$4.00
Ribbon	$39.30
Dowels	$6.00
Command hooks	$4.00
TOTAL	**$53.30**

STORE COST

I haven't seen any vendors offering ribbon wall solutions to the public.

Coneflower Boutonniere

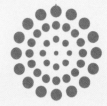

For the gentleman with refined tastes such as your beloved groom, any old boutonniere just won't do. Roses and calla lilies are overdone, and many other flowers are just too flowery to fit his modern aesthetic.

For this boutonniere I wanted to use an unusual flower, one that looked spiky and masculine but that was still beautiful. While trolling the local flower market, I discovered such a bloom: the coneflower. Related to Echinacea, it possesses medicinal as well as decorative purposes. I just adore it! Paired with a bright yellow orchid and dyed purpled integrifolia, it makes a stunning, modern, masculine boutonniere.

Coneflowers are available in peak wedding season, from May through October. Orchids are available year-round, as is most of the dried integrifolia. There are a few places to find integrifolia online, but your best bet is to order it directly from your neighborhood florist. Most, if you ask nicely, will be delighted to place an order for you.

CRAFTY COMMITMENT

1 hour
for 6 boutonnieres

WITH A LITTLE HELP FROM MY FRIENDS

On the big day, hand off the floral arranging to a trusted friend or two while you're off being a beautiful bride.

SUPPLIES

- 1 bunch of coneflowers, also known as *Echinacea purpurea*
- Scissors
- 1 bunch of purple integrifolia, available from florists
- 1 yellow Aranda orchid
- Floral tape
- Ribbon, ¼ in. wide
- Small straight pins
- Pearl-tipped corsage pins

DIRECTIONS

1. Gather together your coneflowers and remove the leaves from the stems. Cut the stems to about 4 in. in length.

2. Cut a stem of integrifolia to about 5 in. in length. Be careful here, as the dye from the foliage can get on everything. Have some paper towels nearby to wipe your fingers. I'm sure your finger-prints are lovely, but they're better suited for identification purposes than as part of your wedding decor.

3. Group all of your flowers and foliage together. The integrifolia looks best in the very back, as the base of the boutonniere. Next bring the coneflower forward and then add in the lovely orchid as an accent. Wrap the stems together with floral tape. Don't be afraid to play around with the arrangement, but don't overthink it. Simple is best.

4. Now cover the tape with ribbon, wrapping from top to bottom. Secure the ribbon on the back side of the bundle with a straight pin.

5. The finished boutonniere can be attached to a lapel with a pearl-tipped corsage pin.

tips & hints

- *Coneflowers sometimes come with flower petals attached. You may use them as is or you may gently pluck the petals from the center cone. It's up to you.*

- *The integrifolia is a dried and dyed foliage. Be careful when handling it; the dye tends to get on fingers and surfaces when you're working with it. Have some paper towels on hand to wipe your fingers.*

- *If any of the guys in your wedding party have a strong aversion to scents, this is a great boutonniere for them. It's virtually scent-free.*

- *A great modern-looking alternative to the coneflower would be the billy button, also known as Craspedia.*

- *I like using ¼-in.-wide ribbon when wrapping boutonniere stems. It's scaled nicely for small florals such as this, but you can use other widths without a problem.*

- *Speaking of ribbon, use any color—or combination of colors—that you like!*

- *This is a project that's best done the day of the wedding. Please hand this off to a trusted helper, with complete instructions, if you've got an already packed morning. (Most of you will.)*

Price Breakdown

YOUR COST

Coneflowers	**$6.50**
Integrifolia	**$7.50**
Orchids	**$7.50**
Floral tape	**$2.00**
Ribbon	**$1.00**
Pins	**$2.00**

TOTAL	**$26.50**

for 4 to 6 boutonnieres or
$4.40 to **$6.60** each

STORE COST

Florists typically charge **$20** or more per boutonniere.

Faux Mercury Glass and Protea Centerpiece

For this project, I wanted to do an interpretation of modern that took something old like mercury glass—a staple in vintage decor—and turned it into something new and fresh by adding a bright-but-unusual flower.

Mercury glass was mass-produced in the late 1800s to early 1930s using a technique that sandwiched a liquid silver nitrate solution between walls of glass in vases and vessels. I love-with-a-capital-L mercury glass because even though it has vintage roots, it looks delightfully industrial and modern. These days it's a highly prized collectable and costs a small fortune to acquire, so of course, I had to seek out a way to DIY it on the cheap.

Essentially, this project involves just adding glue to the inside of a vase, applying silver leaf on top, and finishing it off with several layers of spray paint. That's well within the skill set of even the least crafty of crafters!

Do take note that this project takes several hours—or even days—to complete, so give yourself ample time to allow the glue and the layers of paint to dry completely.

CRAFTY COMMITMENT

24 to 48 hours for the vases; 30 minutes per floral arrangement

WITH A LITTLE HELP FROM MY FRIENDS

On the big day, hand off the floral arranging to a few trusted helpers while you're off being a blissful, beautiful bride.

SUPPLIES

- Glass vase,
  5 in. by 5 in. by 5 in.
- Glass cleaner
  and paper towels
- Silver leaf sizing (sizing
  is glue made specifically
  for silver leaf)
- Silver leaf sheets
- Soft foam brushes
- Krylon® Looking
  Glass® Mirror-Like Paint
- Water
- 5 to 6 protea flowers
- 2 dozen pink
  Veronica flowers
- Heavy-duty floral cutters
  or garden shears

A.

DIRECTIONS

1. Clean the inside of the glass vase with glass cleaner and a paper towel. Let the vase dry completely.

2. Once you have a clean, dry vase, apply a thin layer of silver leaf sizing to the inner walls of the vase and let the sizing dry until the "tacky" stage according to the manufacturer's directions **(drawing A)**.

3. Hold a sheet of silver leaf parallel to the inner wall of the vase and press it gently onto the tacky surface. Use a clean, dry foam brush to press the silver leaf into the corners and flatten down pieces that may be sticking up **(drawing B)**. The silver leaf should be breaking apart at this stage; that's normal and what you want to be seeing. You don't want smooth, perfect surfaces here.

4. Allow the silver leaf to dry, usually overnight.

5. The next step is to apply layers of the spray mirror paint over the top of the silver leaf on the inside of the vase **(photo A)**. This finishes off the vase, giving it a full-coverage coating of silver that will make it look like mercury glass. For this project, it took 6 full coats of the spray paint to get the coverage I wanted. It's important to let each coat dry before adding the next; otherwise you'll end up with weird streaks.

6. After the coats of paint are dry, you may then add your water and protea to the vase. Protea have very thick, woody stems, so you'll need to have a good pair of floral cutters or garden shears on hand to give them a proper trim. Add in sprigs of pink Veronica to fill in any large gaps between protea.

A.

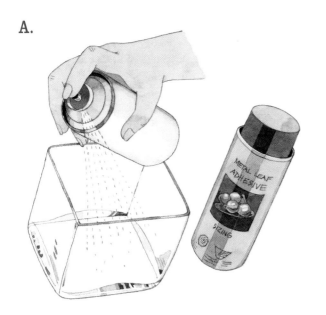

B.

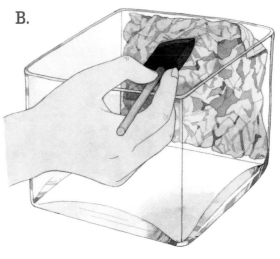

Gently press silver leaf sheet with dry, clean foam brush into corners.

tips & hints

- *Any size or shape of vase can be used for this project. Vases with curves or indentations are harder to do but they can be done, and they look gorgeous.*

- *Not into protea? No problem! Any bright, bold flower will do, really. I like lilies, spiky mums, billy balls (Craspedia), or nearly any tropical flower, as well as succulents, for modern alternatives.*

- *Please do the spray painting outside in an area with plenty of ventilation!*

- *One can of spray covers 2 small vases. Save those craft store coupons and stock up on the silver paint when you can get it at a discount.*

- *The centerpiece looks great set on a mirror with votive candles surrounding it.*

FIT YOUR STYLE

Instead of protea, use beautiful white peonies for a winter wedding or deep red roses for a gorgeous fairy-tale wedding.

Price Breakdown

YOUR COST

Vase	**$8.00**
Foam brushes	**$5.00**
Silver sizing	**$6.00**
Silver leaf sheets	**$7.00**
Krylon Looking Glass Mirror-Like Paint	**$12.00**
Protea (6 stems)	**$35.00**
Pink Veronica	**$8.00**
TOTAL	**$81.00**
	per centerpiece

STORE COST

Florists will charge **$75.00** to **$125.00** for a similar centerpiece.

Resources

Finding the right supplies can make or break a project. I've put together a list of some of my favorite retailers, manufacturers, and websites to help you find all of the supplies called for in this book.

General Craft Stores

Most of the supplies used in the book came from my local big-box craft stores. Many of the biggies frequently offer 40-percent-off to 50-percent-off coupons, making them great resources for quality craft supplies on the cheap.

A. C. MOORE
www.acmoore.com

JO-ANN FABRIC AND CRAFT STORES
www.joann.com

MICHAELS STORES
www.michaels.com

SAVE ON CRAFTS
www.save-on-crafts.com

Fabric & Textiles

DENVER FABRICS
www.denverfabrics.com

SILK BARON
www.silkbaron.com

Crepe Paper

BLUMCHEN
www.blumchen.com

A CASTLE IN THE AIR
www.castleintheair.biz

MISTERART
www.misterart.com

Flowers

These were the top recommendations from my DIY wedding community:

2G ROSES
www.freshroses.com

FIFTY FLOWERS
www.fiftyflowers.com

FLOWERS BY FLOWERBUD.COM
www.flowerbud.com

GROWER'S BOX
www.growersbox.com

Paper & Cardstock

I have a mix of retailers and manufacturers in this category. Although many manufacturers don't sell directly to the public, their websites are an excellent spot to check out what's new and exciting in product offerings. They'll also have lists of retailers where you can find their products. The retail shops have been recommended and reliable sources throughout my entire crafting career.

ANNA GRIFFIN, INC.
www.annagriffin.com

BAZZILL BASICS PAPER, INC.
www.bazzillbasics.com

CRANE & CO.
www.crane.com

DICK BLICK
www.dickblick.com

ENVELOPMENTS
www.envelopments.com

PAPER PRESENTATION
www.paperpresentation.com

PAPER SOURCE
www.paper-source.com

Pinecones

PINECONES OF THE NORTHWEST
www.
pineconesofthenorthwest
.com

WINTER WOODS
www.winterwoods.com

Precious Metal Clay

COOL TOOLS
www.cooltools.us

FIRE MOUNTAIN GEMS AND BEADS
www.firemountaingems
.com

SILVER-CLAY.COM
www.silver-clay.com

WHOLE LOTTA WHIMSY
www.wholelottawhimsy
.com

Ribbon

Great ribbon stores abound online. Check out these fine retailers for beautiful, affordable ribbons in nearly every color imaginable:

C.O.D. WHOLESALE
www.codwholesale.com

M & J TRIMMING
www.mjtrim.com

MIDORI RIBBON
www.midoriribbon.com

PAPER MART
www.papermart.com

THE RIBBON SPOT
www.theribbonspot.com

Rhinestones & Rhinestone Chain

DIAMOND PARTY CONFETTI
www.
diamondpartyconfetti.com

DREAMTIME CREATIONS
www.dreamtimecreations
.com

Rubber Stamps

HERO ARTS
www.heroarts.com

IMPRESS RUBBER STAMPS
www.
impressrubberstamps.com

MAGENTA RUBBER STAMPS
www.magentastyle.com

SIMON'S STAMPS
www.simonstamp.com

Vases, Decor & Glassware

CRATE AND BARREL
www.crateandbarrel.com

EBAY
www.ebay.com

IKEA
www.ikea.com

WEST ELM
www.westelm.com

Index